SPIRAL GUIDE

FUERTEVENTURA

Publishing

Contents

the magazine 5

+ The Desert Island
+ Guanches, Majoreros and Conquistadores
+ Catch a Wave ✦ Carnaval and Fiesta
+ Fiesta ✦ Food and Drink
+ Family Fuerteventura ✦ Meet the Wildlife
+ Life in the Seas ✦ Shipwreck!
+ Did You Know? ✦ My Fuerteventura
+ Superlative Fuerteventura

Finding Your Feet 35

+ First Two Hours
+ Getting Around
+ Accommodation
+ Food and Drink
+ Shopping
+ Entertainment

The North 43

Getting Your Bearings
In Four Days
Don't Miss ✦ Corralejo ✦ Isla de Lobos ✦ La Oliva
At Your Leisure ✦ 4 more places to explore
Where to...✦ Eat and Drink ✦ Stay ✦ Shop
+ Be Entertained

The Centre 65

Getting Your Bearings
In Two Days
Don't Miss ✦ Betancuria ✦ Antigua
+ Ecomuseo de La Alcogida
At Your Leisure ✦ 9 more places to explore
Where to... ✦ Eat and Drink ✦ Stay ✦ Shop
+ Be Entertained

The South 85

Getting Your Bearings
In Three Days
Don't Miss ✦ Playas de Jandia ✦ La Lajita Oasis Park
At Your Leisure ✦ 5 more places to explore
Where to... ✦ Eat and Drink ✦ Stay ✦ Shop
✦ Be Entertained

Lanzarote 107

Finding Your Feet
Getting Your Bearings
In One Day
Don't Miss ✦ Parque Nacional Timanfaya
✦ Jameos del Agua ✦ Teguise
At Your Leisure ✦ 9 more places to explore
Where to... ✦ Eat and Drink ✦ Shop

Gran Canaria 127

Finding Your Feet
Getting Your Bearings
Don't Miss ✦ Casa de Colón ✦ Museo Canario
At Your Leisure ✦ 3 more places to explore
Where to... ✦ Eat and Drink ✦ Shop

Walks and Drives 137

✦ Isla de Lobos
✦ Sendero de Bayuyo Volcanoes
✦ Northern and Central Highlights
✦ Coast-to-Coast

Practicalities 153

✦ Before You Go ✦ When to Go
✦ When You Are There

Useful Words and Phrases 159

Atlas 161

Index 171

Written by Paul Murphy
Produced by Cambridge Publishing Management Ltd, Cambridge,
England
Updated by Paul Murphy
Update managed by Bookwork Creative Associates

Published by AA Publishing, a trading name of Automobile Association
Developments Limited, whose registered office is
Fanum House, Basing View, Basingstoke, Hampshire RG21 4EA.
Registered number 1878835.

ISBN: 978-0-7495-4741-7

A CIP catalogue record for this book is available from the British Library

Cover design and binding style by permission of AA Publishing
Colour separation by Leo Reprographics
Printed and bound in China by Leo Paper Products

Find out more about AA Publishing and the wide range of services the
AA provides by visiting our website at www.theAA.com/travel

A03439 Mapping © KOMPASS-Karten GmbH, A-6063
Rum/Innsbruck

the magazine

The Desert

Of all the Canaries, Fuerteventura is the classic desert island. It is often referred to as "a little bit of Sahara which has chipped off the coast of Africa", and while that is geologically incorrect – like all the Canaries it was born from underwater volcanic explosions – it does convey a good deal of the character of Fuerteventura. And of course the island's golden sands *are* from the Sahara, blown across as dust particles over the millennia.

For visitors much of the island offers a magnificent untamed natural beauty: ancient mountain ranges and volcanic cones trimmed by deep dry *barrancos* (ravines), and coastlines either softened by Saharan dunes or battered by the elements into bizarre shapes. Less attractively, there are also great stretches of volcanic *malpais* (literally, badlands), black areas of scorched, cracked earth where nothing more than lichens grow. In neighbouring Lanzarote they have managed to turn similar adversity to good purpose but here geological conditions are different and this option is not available. For the islanders, certainly before the advent of tourism, this has always been a harsh, unforgiving climate in which to eke a living.

Wind is a powerful resource and (above) goats are prized

Island

However, *majoreros*, as the people of Fuerteventura are colloquially known, are nothing if not resourceful. In the fields the wind has been harnessed to power hundreds of *molinos* (conventional windmills), *molinas* (windmills mounted on top of buildings), steel water pumps and wind turbines, while the fierce sun ripens the famous Canary tomatoes exported

Despite the harsh terrain, farmers eke out a living on the land

Where is everyone?

With an average population density of just 12 people per square kilometre, Fuerteventura is easily the emptiest of the Canary Islands. Much of the island's west coast is deserted and accessible only by tracks, and the northern part of the Jandia peninsula is unpopulated except for the single ramshackle hamlet of Cofete. This is good news for naturists and away from the resorts most beaches are "clothing optional".

being poverty-stricken but today the beaches of Corralejo are filled with visitors who spend hundreds of euros on kiteboarding courses, enjoy slap-up meals in the town's many restaurants and then retire to be pampered in luxury at their four- and five-star hotels.

Having managed to survive on a basic economy since before the days of the Conquest, the islanders' latest challenge is how to reap the benefits of tourism without sowing the seeds of cultural destruction. The success of *casas rurales* and *hoteles rurales* (rural guesthouses and hotels), as well as projects such as the Ecomuseo de La Alcogida open-air museum, are seen by many to be the most appropriate routes for controlled tourist development. Yet the growing number of holiday resorts at El Cotillo and Corralejo, not to mention the plans for hollowing out the island's most sacred mountain as a tourist attraction, are of great concern to many islanders and Canarian conservationists. For the moment, at least, most of Fuerteventura remains, in the words of the poet Miguel Unamuno, "an oasis in the desert of civilization".

Tourism has brought new life to the island

from here to northern Europe. It is no wonder that goats are so prized in a landscape that would support few other kinds of fussier creature – until quite recently, that most durable of all land animals, the camel, was a familiar island workhorse.

Fishermen in particular are at the mercy of the elements – the often-visible wrecks of ocean-going vessels weighing many thousands of tons are testimony to the power of the Atlantic – and on the west coast the fishing fleets operate only during the summer season.

Yet times are changing. A 1960s guidebook to Lanzarote referred to Fuerteventura as

Langostas on the menu

It is not only sand that blows across from the Sahara. Migratory birds are blown off course and end up here along with swarms of locusts (*langostas*). Millions descended on the island in 2004, and while they are harmless to humans directly, they do of course devastate crops, and have a deterrent effect on tourism. It is possible to turn the tables on these voracious creatures, however, and official leaflets distributed in 2004 on how to deal with the creatures even included a couple of recipes – apparently they are quite tasty when fried in garlic!

Guanches, Majoreros and Conquistadores

Conquistador Jean de Béthencourt came to the island in 1402

When the Norman baron Jean de Béthencourt first arrived on Fuerteventura in 1402, a curious sight awaited him. Here were a people only slightly removed from the Stone Age in appearance and technology. They lived together, just a few hundred strong, in primitive societies with basic laws and rough draconian justice; convicted criminals' skulls were crushed by heavy rocks, for example. Yet it is also recorded that they were a peaceful people with high moral standards; Béthencourt's priests chronicled, "go throughout the world and nowhere will you find a finer and better formed people…with great minds were they to receive instructions" (Bontier & le Verrier, tr. and ed, *Le Canarien*, 1872). The history books came to call them Guanches ("gwanches") but in fact this term is a general

What's in a name?

The island's original name was Erbania, probably referring to the wall (*bani* in the Berber language) that divided the kingdoms. The first mention of Forte Ventura appears on a map in 1339. Popular legend has it that when Béthencourt landed he uttered the words, "Que fuerte ventura", "What great fortune (luck)". But more prosaically it probably refers to the island's strong winds.

one for any aboriginal Canary Island dweller and the ancient people of Fuerteventura came to be known as *majoreros* (pronounced "ma-ho-rair-os") or Mahohreros, possibly named after the particular types of caves (*majos*) that they built, or from the word *mahos* meaning a type of goatskin shoe which they wore.

The origin of the Guanches

It is thought that these original islanders were of Berber origin, coming from Morocco in Roman times (carbon-dating points to the 1st or 2nd century BC) and they may have been from the Canarii tribe, hence the subsequent name of the archipelago. They dwelt in caves and in low houses (as many villagers do today), kept goats, ate shellfish and grain, made simple pottery and tattooed themselves in geometrical patterns with pottery stamps known as *pintaderas*. These were probably also used to distinguish ownership of pots in grain stores.

The island was divided into two kingdoms: Jandía (as it is today), ruled by King Guize, and Maxorata (the rest of the island), ruled by King Ayoze. Béthencourt recorded that a low wall, around a metre high, crossed the island at La Pared dividing the two kingdoms. Traces of it can still be found today and there may have been defensive turrets in place.

An early slave trader's chronicles recorded, "The natives of Fuerteventura are few in number and live on meat and milk, and are of great stature, men and women alike, and are very firm in their beliefs [in ancient deities]. And it is very hard to take them alive." (Bontier & le Verrier, tr. and ed. *Le Canarien*, 1872).

Béthencourt had arrived on the islands with two main objectives. His first was to discover from where the fabled "River of Gold" traffic

Native Fuerteventuran islanders were known as Majoreros and mostly lived in caves

Spain's gain

If the French court had backed Jean de Béthencourt's adventures, Canary Islanders today might be speaking French instead of Spanish. The French refused to finance him so the Norman knight took his proposal to Castile who accepted on condition that the conquered territories should become part of their territories.

Traces of the Majoreros today

It is often claimed that Fuerteventura is the richest of all the Canary Islands, as far as evidence of its aboriginal people is concerned, yet the vast majority of these are hidden away or inaccessible to the average visitor. Objects found in the cave at Villaverde may be seen in the Museo Arqueológico y Etnográfico at Betancuria (► 72) but the best-known site associated with the ancients is Montaña Tindaya (► 57).

was pouring out of the Sahara. His second was to convert the natives to Christianity. Frustrated in meeting either of these aims and meeting strong resistance from the islanders, the French nobleman sailed back to his Castilian sponsors for reinforcements. When Béthencourt returned with his conquistadors in 1404 he found that the islanders had built forts at Valtarajal (later known as Betancuria) and Rico Roque (close to El Cotillo), but armed with merely spears and staves against guns they were soon overcome. Some fled into the mountains before giving themselves up to be sold into slavery abroad. Many died of common diseases imported by the invaders. In January 1405, the two kings surrendered and the remaining islanders followed their example. They were allowed to live and the kings were even given part of their lands back. However, Fuerteventura was now an outpost of Castile.

Mysterious "podomorphs" discovered on Montaña Tindaya

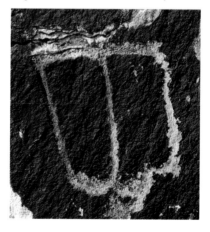

CATCH A WAVE

Ask anyone who has ever ridden a board across the waves and they will tell you Fuerteventura is one of the best places in the world for windsurfing.

It's basically down to geography. The Canary Islands have always benefited (and suffered) from heavy swells and strong winds. Ancient mariners relied on these "trade winds" to speed their voyages, and water sports fans also look for strong and reliable breezes. This is where the "acceleration zones" come in. These occur where the wind

is funnelled between mountains or small islands and can triple the wind in strength. Because of its location, Fuerteventura – in particular the Sotavento coast of Jandía and the northern coast around Corralejo – benefits from this effect.

Windsurfing is the number one sport on the island and in July 1986 the first Windsurfing World Cup competition was held on Sotavento Beach. In 2001, it became the Windsurfing and Kiteboarding World Cup in recognition of this exciting new development in water sports. Kitesurfing or kiteboarding began in its present form in the late 1990s and has been described as a cross between windsurfing, wakeboarding and paragliding. Kitesurfers control a wing of lightweight fabric, which pulls them across the water at speeds of up to 70kph (43mph). The experts can fly up to 15m (50ft) high in the air performing all manner of gymnastics before coming down again some 70m (76yds) from where they first took off.

How do I get started ?
Windsurfing
A couple of hours spent typically in a quiet waist-deep lagoon setting will set you back around €60. A three-day course will cost around €120. After that you should have an idea if you like it or not and can sign on for progressively longer courses and/or hire your own rig (board and sail).

The wind and waves are perfect for water sports (left)

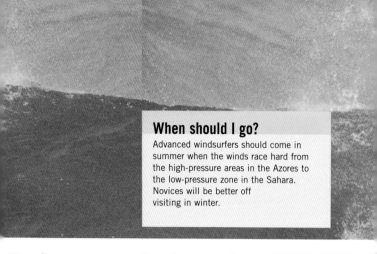

When should I go?

Advanced windsurfers should come in summer when the winds race hard from the high-pressure areas in the Azores to the low-pressure zone in the Sahara. Novices will be better off visiting in winter.

Kitesurfing

Despite what you may think, you don't have to be a surfer of any kind to start kitesurfing, though of course it helps. In fact it's more important at the outset that you can handle a stunt kite properly and understand the nature of the wind. Neither do you need a great deal of strength, as the harness will take the strain off your arms. An introductory eight-hour course costs around €220.

Top Operators

Flag Beach Windsurf and Kitesurf Centre, Corralejo (►64)

Pro Center René Egli K2 Watersports Centre, Sotavento Beach, Jandia (►106)

Surfing

Fuerteventura is also renowned for its surfing conditions, which are best during the winter months (October to March) when there is less wind and the waves are bigger. Islandboarders are the only BSA (British Surfing Association) recognized

Surfers of all kinds flock here

centre on Fuerteventura. A division of Flag Beach Windsurf Centre (➤ 13), they have 17 years experience. A one-day course costs €45 and consists of a four-hour session involving safety, paddling and standing techniques. The beginner's course (€110) aims to have you standing after three days. You will spend three to four hours in the water everyday learning standing techniques, board control, paddling and wipe out survival, plus theory lessons on types of breaks, surf-board design, equipment, history and water survival and safety. You can then enroll on a three-day intermediate course, also for €110. Contact www.islandboarderssurf school.com.

Another reputable school is Quiksilver Surf School, also based at Corralejo. It was founded in 1994 by Joachim Hirsch, German longboard champion in 1999 and former member of the German national surf team – see www.quiksilver-surfschool. com.

Unless you're a born surf dude, bank on a few days' instruction and hard physical work before you see any benefits. After around five years you'll be ready to take on stretches such as the Suicides, the Shooting Gallery or Acid Break.

Experienced surfers should check out the article by Nick Ajose on www.fuerteventura. com/surfing.

Water sports schools are dotted along the coast

Carnaval and Fiesta

The Canary Islands celebrate the traditional pre-Lent carnival, or *carnaval* as it is known in Spain, with every ounce of energy they can muster. Gran Canaria and Tenerife compete to stage the biggest parades this side of Rio, while the other islands do their very best to keep pace.

The biggest *carnaval* celebrations on Fuerteventura are in Corralejo and Puerto del Rosario, though it is celebrated with gusto all over the island. The dates vary from year to year but it all starts around nine weeks before Easter (usually early to mid-February) with the *Verbena de la Sábana* (Sheet Party) for which participants dress in a sheet and little else. After this the Carnival Queen and the Children's Queen are elected. The climax of

Carnaval is celebrated all over the island

festivities is the Friday before Shrove Tuesday, when the Carnival Drag Queen is chosen, and the next day, when the grand parade of dozens of colourful floats takes place. Street parties and processions shimmy and shake to the insistent beat of salsa, lubricated by a seemingly inexhaustible supply of *cuba libre* (rum, cola, lime juice and ice) served from street kiosks.

A feature of *carnaval* is that men always dress in drag. If you think that is odd wait until you see the strangest ceremony of all, the Burial of the Sardine, which symbolises the end of *carnaval* and the beginning of Lent, as well as the Lenten fast and abstinence. On Ash Wednesday a huge papier-maché sardine is carried in mock funeral procession through the streets accompanied by the bizarre sight and sound of black-clad "mourners" wailing and crying. When the sardine arrives at its appointed place at the harbour, fireworks inside the fish are lit and it is literally blown to pieces.

Everyone puts on fancy dress and parties in the street

Tips

If you know you will be in Fuerteventura during *carnaval* time be prepared to party and bring along some fancy dress – anything will do, the more colourful and more outlandish the better.

If you really want to see how Canarians can celebrate *carnaval* catch a plane to Las Palmas (► 128–129)

See www.fuerteventura.com for dates and details of events.

Island fiestas commemorate the feast day of the local saint or the Virgin/Our Lady, (*Nuestra Señora*). The centrepiece is a procession with prominent parishioners carrying an effigy of the saint or the Virgin shoulder-high through the streets accompanied by troupes of local musicians in traditional dress. The more important fiestas will also have carnival-style floats, street food and stalls, and culminate in fireworks. One of the island's most important fiestas is the Romería (pilgrimage) to the Ermita of

FIESTA

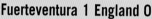

Fuerteventura 1 England 0

On 13 October the locals celebrate the day they gave the English a bloody nose in 1740 by re-enacting the Battle of Tamasite, near Tuineje. A troop of well-armed English privateers (state-sanctioned pirates) attacked near Tuineje and was seen off by a group of 37 locals with muskets and agricultural tools. Thirty Englishmen were killed and five locals died. A cannon was captured and is on display outside the archaeological museum in Betancuría. A painting in the church of Tuineje also recalls the victory.

the Virgen de la Peña, the patron saint of the island, in Vega de Río Palmas on the third weekend in September.

The Fiesta de Nuestra Señora del Carmen on 16 July at Corralejo and Morro Jable pays homage to the patron saint of fishermen with colourful boat processions led by local fishermen carrying a statue of the Virgin.

On the third Sunday in August, the old harbour at El Cotillo is dotted with boats celebrating Nuestra Señora del Buen Viaje.

From pilgrimages to flotillas of boats, there are fiestas all year round

Food and Drink

Genuine Canarian cuisine is all about dishes that originated in the kitchens of peasants and fishermen, as typified by hearty stews and simple barbecued fish. International and particularly anglicised meals may be the staple menu in resorts such as Caleta de Fuste, Jandía Playa and the new part of Corralejo, but thankfully the majority of restaurants on the island still serve a mix of Spanish and Canarian food. Start off with tapas, a concept imported from the Spanish mainland, and you have a meal that is as interesting, colourful and satisfying as in any European holiday destination.

Mojo and papas

The Canary Islands' most distinctive tastes are *mojo picón* and *mojo verde*. *Mojo picón* (literally "piquant sauce") is made from chilli peppers, garlic, cumin, paprika and vinegar. It is served cold and normally accompanies meat dishes and *papas arrugadas*. The latter (literally "wrinkly potatoes") is another Canarian staple – small new potatoes boiled in salty water and served with a

Spanish dishes such as pinchos (above) and paella (below) are available widely

generous sprinkling of sea salt. They are nearly always delicious and rarely taste too salty. By contrast to the fiery red variety, *mojo verde* (green sauce) is a cool fresh blend substituting coriander for chilli, and always accompanies fish.

Island specials: meat and cheese

The goat is the symbol of Fuerteventura (► 24–25) and appears on the menu in just about every conceivable form. Most local restaurants have goat's cheese (*queso de cabra*) among their starters, usually with sliced tomatoes. It may also be fried in breadcrumbs and served with quince jam (*membrillo*), palm honey (*miel de palma*) or perhaps *mojo verde*. Look under "specialities" for *cabrito* (kid), which is either fried, baked or served in a stew (*compuesta*). Another goat dish is *hígado de cabra frita* (fried goat liver). Some restaurants only serve goat or kid stew on a Sunday

lunchtime and specify that it must be ordered in advance. *Conejo* (rabbit) is also popular, served either in a tomato stew (*al salmorejo*) or perhaps fried (*frito*).

South American specials

Steaks from Argentina are very popular. Specialist meat restaurants may also serve Argentine sausage, rolled beef and pork steaks. A few cafés sell *arepas*, spicy pasties from Venezuela, while an Italian restaurant in Corralejo serves Argentine toffee pastries for dessert!

Island fish

The cheapest fish on most local restaurant menus is *corvina* (black drum) but it's usually worth paying a bit more for *cherne* (grouper), *vieja* (parrotfish), *sama* (sea bream) or *gallo* (John Dory). Other local fish and seafood items include *atún* (tuna), *pez espada* (swordfish), *merluza* (hake) and *lenguado* (sole). Ever popular is that

Buying fresh produce at the market is much more fun than visiting the supermarket

sizzling Spanish starter *gambas al ajillo* (prawns in garlic and spicy tomato sauce). Paella, Spain's national dish, typically including mussels, prawns and often rabbit, is very popular.

Sweet things

In traditional local establishments the choice of *postres* (desserts) is usually restricted to flan (the ubiquitous Spanish crème caramel) or *helado* (ice cream). However, in the new wave of Spanish-Canarian restaurants keep an eye out for some of the following: home-made cheesecake; home-made apple cake; *frangollo* (made of *gofio* – see opposite – and dried fruit soaked in syrup); *bienmesabe* (ground almonds, egg yolks and sugar syrup blended to the consistency of honey), often served with ice cream or bananas; *leche asada* (literally "baked milk", a kind of lemony sponge milk pudding); and *leche frita* ("fried milk"), also like crème caramel.

Vegetarian vicissitudes

Fish aside, it's hard to get a true vegetarian meal in a local restaurant. Even dishes like *potaje de berros* (watercress soup) or *garbanzos compuestos* (chickpea stew) include bacon or pork. The best bet is the newer breed of restaurants, many of which make a point of offering interesting Spanish or locally inspired vegetarian dishes.

Gofio – the staff of life

Gofio, flour made by grinding toasted barley, maize or wheat, has been the Canarian staple since Guanche times (▶ 9–11). It is typically eaten by islanders as porridge or as a kind of polenta, or used to thicken soups and stews. It also occasionally finds its way onto the tourist menu under *gofio escaldado* (combined with fish stock), *helado de gofio* (ice cream) or perhaps *mousse de gofio*.

And to drink…

Fuerteventura produces small quantities of its own wine but most table wine is from mainland Spain or Lanzarote. The latter is invariably the island's famous *malvasia*. Try also *ronmiel* ("honey rum"), a Canarian speciality made with palm honey.

Snacking

Go into even the humblest corner café and they will be pleased to serve you a satisfying *bocadillo de lomo* (pork loin sandwich in French bread), which automatically comes with cheese and tomato. The best coffee is usually Italian (rather than Spanish), look out for the Tonino Lamborghini brand.

More Canarian specialities

Potaje or *puchero canario* – a hearty meat and vegetable casserole, which may be served with *gofio* dumplings.

Rancho canario – a stew of meat, potatoes, chickpeas, tomatoes and noodles.

Ropa vieja – literally "old clothes", a stew of meat, chickpeas and whatever vegetables the chef throws in.

Sancocho – salt fish and potato stew.

Local Canarian wines (above)

Stop for a tapas snack (top left)

Presentation helps to whet the appetite (bottom left)

Tasty tapas and starters

Albóndigas (meatballs)

Calamares (fried battered squid)

Chorizos al vino tinto (paprika sausage in red wine)

Croquetas (croquettes, which may be filled with potatoes)

Gambas (prawns)

Jamón serrano (mountain cured ham). *Pata negra* is the best variety, though very expensive.

Mejillones (mussels)

Pimientos (peppers). These may be stuffed with a variety of fillings. *Pimientos de pardón* are the hot spicy variety. They are sometimes served smothered in melted cheese.

Pulpo (octopus)

Tortilla (potato omelette)

Family
Fuerteventura

With its mile upon mile of sandy beaches, Fuerteventura is a delight for young children and perfect for older ones who may wish to start their first water sports lessons here.

Windsurfing
Children's windsurfing tuition begins at ten years old. Flag Beach in the north (►64), René Egli in the south (►106), and Fanatic Fun Centre in Caleta de Fuste are recommended operators. Beginners are taught in calm lagoon conditions: at Risco del Paso in the south; at El Cotillo in the north; and on the calm beach of Caleta de Fuste.

Surfing
Bodyboarding, or boogie boarding as it is also known, is the first step towards learning to surf, and kids can start this as soon as they are confident in the water. Shops all over the island sell bodyboards. The only sandy beaches where surfboarding can be practiced, however, are in the north, at El Cotillo and

Kids can have fun by the sea, ride a camel and see some tropical birds

Visitor attractions
If your children enjoy seeing birds and animals – there are also shows and camel rides – then Oasis Park at La Lajita (►93–95) is a perfect day out in a tropical garden setting. The island's only water park is in Corralejo at the Baku complex (►49), which also includes a whole host of other family entertainments.

There are tenpin bowling alleys at Caleta de Fuste and at Corralejo.

Flag Beach. Good surfboarding schools are Islandboarders and Quiksilver Surf School, both at Corralejo, and tuition for children begins at the age of ten years.

Scuba-diving

The minimum age for diving is ten years old. Recommended schools in Corralejo are Corralejo Dive Centre and the Punta Amanay Dive Centre (► 27).

Away from it all

Isla de Lobos (► 51–52) is an excellent day out for children. Older ones can be desert island explorers following the signposts, past lagoons, to the lighthouse then up a mini-mountain. Little ones can play safely in the warm shallows of a soft golden sandy cove.

Go fly a kite

Second only in colour to Carnaval is the International Kite Festival which has been held in the dunes of Corralejo on the second weekend of October each year since 1992. The best kite fliers in Europe take part and the highlight is the Night Fly on Saturday night when illuminated kites create a mesmerising performance. Anyone can join in on the Friday when expert instructors are on hand. Just bring a kite – the more colourful the better – and you will be very welcome.

Beware the sun

If you need parasols, lounge beds, snack bars, showers and toilets on the beach, then there's only a limited choice of where to go. Corralejo, Caleta de Fuste, Costa Calma and Morro Jable are well-equipped popular family choices. Many beaches have few facilities so go prepared and always have your own shade to hand. The best beaches for little ones are Playa de la Concha at Isla de Lobos and the lagoon beaches at El Cotillo.

Churches

Visiting churches might not win you a popularity award with the kids but they will probably enjoy viewing the graphic Judgement Day painting which are a feature of most. The Iglesia de Santa María in Betancuria is particularly amusing, with a pumpkin-like monster eating the poor souls in hell.

MEET THE WILDLIFE

Fuerteventura may not have a great choice of indigenous animals but there are three local creatures that almost every visitor will meet!

If Fuerteventura has a national animal it is the goat (*cabra*). These hardy creatures can scavenge a meal from the meanest terrain, from thorny bushes in rocky outcrops to scrubby foliage among the sand dunes. They total around 60,000 strong, almost as many as the island's resident human population. Goats have been herded since Guanche times and at one time or another most parts of this creature have been put to some practical use. Goat meat and cheese feature prominently on all local restaurant menus, their skins were once used for clothing and their stomachs were used for bags in which *gofio* (► 21) was stored.

There are around 300 camels on the island...

Beware leaping goats!

Traffic signs that seem to depict a graceful leaping deer in a red triangle are in fact warning you to beware of the goats. The reason that the sign bears little resemblance to a goat is that it was designed with deer in mind and the Fuerteventura authorities simply bought them "off-the-peg" as the nearest thing!

In total there are more than 30 different types of goats on the island. These range from the plain *blanca* (white) and *negro* (black) varieties to the dapple-coated *puipana colorada*, and from cute little kids to huge spiral-horned beasts. La Rosita at Villaverde (► 56) is a good place to check them out.

Camels

The camel, or rather the single-humped dromedary, was introduced to the island in 1405 by the Normans and, being the most efficient creature in this harsh dry terrain, was used in the fields and as a beast of burden right up until the 1950s. In the 16th century there were 4,000 camels on Fuerteventura, but by 1985 there were less than 30. Nowadays, thanks to tourism and the breeding scheme at Oasis Park (► 93–95), numbers have recovered to around 300 and Oasis Park has plans to set up the first camel milk dairy in Europe. Camel milk has as much protein but 40 per cent less cholesterol than cow's milk, a high mineral and vitamin C content, and is believed to be good for the liver and the complexion. You can ride camels at Oasis Park and La Rosita.

Barbary ground squirrels

Erroneously described as chipmunks, these cute little critters look like a cross between a chipmunk and a grey squirrel and can be seen scuttling almost anywhere on the island where food is being handed out, be it on the promenade in Morro Jable or at the *miradores* of the interior. They are good fun and very tame but it's really not a good idea to feed them as, among other things, this interferes with their natural food-gathering instincts.

...and more than 30 different kinds of goat!

Life in the Seas

The climate, clear volcanic sea beds and depths of up to 3,500m (11,500 feet) make the Canarian archipelago ideal for diving and deep-sea fishing.

Huge "trophy" fish can often be seen on the quayside at Caleta de Fuste, and the Puerto del Rosario deep-sea fishing championship claims to be the biggest of its kind in Europe. There is an enormous variety of fish to be caught, including rays, sharks, swordfish, albacora, big-eye, yellow fin and skipjack tuna, bonito, barracuda, wahoo, and the most prestigious and feistiest prize of all, blue marlin. No previous experience is required and beginners will be heartened to learn that a world record Mako shark (488kg/1,073lb) – since surpassed – was caught by an Englishman who claimed never to have held a fishing rod in his life! All catches belong to the skipper, though most big-game fish are tagged and released. A day's deep-sea fishing, which usually lasts around six hours, costs around €50 per person and there are operators on the quaysides at Caleta de Fuste, Corralejo and Morro Jable.

Whale and dolphin spotting

While it is feasible to spot whales, dolphins, flying fish and turtles on any sea voyage from Fuerteventura, there are two trips dedicated to spotting these creatures. Dolphin Safari is a fast, small deep-sea fishing boat that operates out of Corralejo (tel: 686 725 327 or visit their kiosk on the harbour). Oceanarium Explorer (► 84) is a much larger, family-oriented operation that uses the biggest catamaran on the island. They claim to spot dolphin and whales (on average) on 40 per cent of

You can go game fishing or whale and dolphin spotting

trips, and sea turtles on 95 per cent of trips.

Diving

All operators offer beginner's courses and cater for experienced divers. Angel sharks and rays are the top sights. Recommended operators are Corralejo Dive Centre (tel: 928 535 906, www.divecentrecorralejo.com) and Punta Amanay Dive Centre (tel: 928 535 357, www.punta-amanay.com). The Corralejo Dive Centre is the longest-established on the island, with more than 25 years' experience and over 30 dive sites. There are many other good operators.

The minimum age for diving is usually 10 or 12 years old.

Snorkelling safaris

If you don't want to take the plunge you can simply float on the surface and observe.

There are two "snorkelling safaris" on the island: AquaVentura at Caleta de Fuste (tel: 630 16 76, mob: 618 309 115, www.aquaventura.biz); and Get Wet Snorkel Safari at Corralejo (mob: 646 031 588 or 660 778 053). Both offer the opportunity to spot dolphins, turtles and rays. After a fun high-speed boat ride to the dive site in an

inflatable, you don a wetsuit and follow a guide to places where marine life is regularly sighted. Get Wet visit Isla de Lobos. Trips last between two and four hours in total with around an hour actually snorkelling. Both accept children as young as eight and you don't have to be a strong swimmer, as your wetsuit will help you to float.

Glass-bottomed boats make a tour of Isla de Lobos (► 51–52) and there are two bona-fide submarines. The Subsea Explorer at Caleta de Fuste is part of the Oceanarium Explorer package (► 84), while in the south the Subcat is based at Jandía (www.excursionsonline.com).

Other recommended English-speaking operators include Abyss Divers in Corralejo (mob: 638 722 297, www.abyss-fuerteventura.com). Recommended German-run schools include Deep Blue at Costa Caleta (tel: 928 163 712, www.deep-blue-diving.com), Felix Diving Center at Jandía (tel: 54 14 18, www.tauchen-fuerteventura.com) and Easy-Diving at Costa Calma (tel: 928 876 305, www.easy-diving.net).

Take a snorkelling safari or go diving to see sharks and rays

SHIPWRECK!

The crashing waves and high winds which fuel the island's extreme water sports can mean disaster for commercial shipping, and over the last two decades Fuerteventura has seen many wrecks. Fortunately, only a few lives have been lost and wrecks that have happened close to shore have become sightseeing attractions.

In 1987, the *Rose of Sharon*, a 37m (121 feet) two-masted wooden schooner, built in 1936, washed up on the sands of Jandía and remained there for several years,

becoming the archetypal desert island shipwreck. It became an unofficial island symbol, even appearing on the front cover of tourist brochures. In 1995 the somewhat less picturesque 100m (328 feet) container ship *Jucar* broke up on the shore of Aguas Verdes. In 1999 the *FV Massira*, a deep-sea fishing vessel, went ashore north of El Cotillo and became a popular tourist attraction.

The biggest and most spectacular wreck of all was the SS *American Star*, which between 1993 and 2007 reigned supreme as the island's unofficial number one sight. On a darker note, many boats packed with illegal immigrants from West Africa

A painting of the SS *American Star* (above) and a momento rescued from the sea (below)

have recently been dashed on the rocks with many fatalities. And accidents continue to happen, even close to shore. In 2007 an environmental protection vessel went to Davy Jones' Locker in Corralejo harbour – fortunately there were no deaths.

SS *American Star*

Launched in 1939 as a luxury cruise liner capable of carrying more than 1,200 passengers, and measuring a mighty 220m (723 feet) by 28m (93 feet), the ship spent the war on troop-carrying duty, then resumed transatlantic cruises until 1963 when she began a new life carrying emigrants from the UK to Australia. In 1993 she was sold off, to be towed to Thailand and used as a floating hotel.

The shortest and easiest route was via the Suez Canal. However, it appears her owners chose not to pay the Canal fees and instead made the fatal decision to go along the African coast during storm season. She beached some 100m (110 yards) off the west coast of Fuerteventura at Playa de Garcey and soon split in two.

Within days of the wreck occurring it is said that half the island's inhabitants had paid her a visit and taken away a "souvenir", though none went so far as the owners of the Café El Naufragio who "salvaged" whole cabin sections which can now been seen in Puerto del Rosario (► 75). While there were no deaths as a direct result of the shipwreck there were eight subsequent fatalities, including a man who attempted to swim out to the wreck and was apparently drawn into the chasm at the break; two

treasure seekers met a tragic end when the section they were exploring collapsed beneath them, and another poor soul ended his life by jumping into the sea from the bow section.

Salvaged ship cabins and signs can be seen at Café El Naufragio in Puerto del Rosario

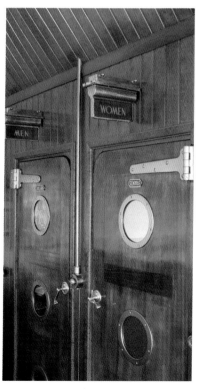

DID YOU KNOW?

Fuerteventura is thought by some to be part of
the mythical landmass of Atlantis.

**Ajuy was the very first point of the whole
Canarian archipelago to surface from the
waters millions of years ago. Walk along the
cliff tops some 100m (328 feet) above sea
level, and the fine fossilised sand that you see
among the rocks was once the beach.**

*The whole island has in fact tilted on an east-west
axis which is why, in general, the west coast is
rocky and the east coast is flat.*

***According to island photographer and historic
researcher Jo Hammer, the ancient
Fuerteventurans (Majos) built spiral temples of
lava stone and each had a statue holding a ball
in the middle. These Efequén, as they were called,
were destroyed by the Spanish.***

That the island's holy mountain, Mount Tindaya,
may soon have its "heart" removed to make way
for an art installation. Plans to hollow out a cube
the height of a ten-storey building will make it
one of the largest underground caverns ever
constructed.

My Fuerteventura

Fuerteventura has a laid-back lifestyle all its own. Two "foreigners" who run very successful tourist businesses here give their views, along with a true *majorero*, whose mission is to preserve his island's identity.

Animal magic: Maria Lazaga Romero

Five years ago Maria Lazaga Romero was a successful lawyer in her hometown of Las Palmas, but gave it up to manage La Lajita Oasis Park (► 93–95) in the backwoods of Fuerteventura. During Maria's four years as general manager the park has become one of the biggest tourist attractions in the Canaries. Maria's colleagues constantly interrupt us but she insists, "here, when I leave work I have no stress. I walk and swim at Tarajalejo or Risco El Paso, you see only the birds and sea."

Surf's up: Ben Thomas

Also born in Gran Canaria but with his formative years spent in Cornwall, Ben Thomas moved to Fuerteventura in 1985 and is the owner of Flag Beach Windsurf and Kitesurf Centre, the biggest water sports operator in the north of the island (► 64). "When I came here there was virtually nothing. I was a pioneer and I believe I am still the only 'foreigner' who has been granted a beach concession in Fuerteventura, if not the whole archipelago."

My land, my country: Tinín Martínez

Tinín Martínez is president of the environmental group Mahoh, which means "my land/my country". The movement came into being at the beginning of the 1980s as a response to proposed building on the sand dunes of Corralejo. After much campaigning by Mahoh, the dunes were declared a national park. Since then 13 other areas of the island have also been declared National Protected Spaces. "Twenty years ago I did not oppose development, as long as it was sensitive development," recalls Tinín, "but today I am campaigning for a full stop until we have caught up with what is currently underway. We must learn the mistakes of the coast and conserve the interior".

Both locals and foreigners have found success in tourism

SUPERLATIVE
FUERTEVENTURA

Best beaches for children
- Lagos (lagoon) beaches, El Cotillo (► 55)
- Playa la Concha, Isla de Lobos (► 51–52)

Best wild beaches
- Playa del Castillo and Playa del Aljibe de la Cueva, both at El Cotillo; Cofete. (It is not safe to swim at Cofete.)

Best water sports operators
- North: Flag Beach at Corralejo (► 64)
- South: René Egli at Sotavento (► 104)

Best family day out
- La Lajita Oasis Park (► 93–95)

Best views
- From Montaña de la Caldera on Isla de Lobos: views of three islands

○ From Mirador de la Morro, Betancuria: sweeping panoramas of the Betancuria National Park

○ Volcan de Bayuyo: looking down into Corralejo's "backyard" and across to Isla de Lobos and Lanzarote

Five atmospheric restaurants

○ Casa de Santa María, Betancuria (►79)

○ Don Antonio, Vega de Río Palmas (►81)

○ El Camello, La Pared (►100)

○ Hotel Rural Mahoh, Villaverde (►62)

○ El Veril, El Cotillo (►59)

The perfect little café

○ Inside the Museo Artesanía in the Casa Santa María in Betancuria (►79)

The oldest "room"

○ Used as a Guanche dwelling, El Llano cave at Villaverde (►56) was formed around one million years ago

Best museum

○ The Ecomuseo de La Alcogida at Tefía (►74) is not just a collection of dusty objects, but the story of everyday life of the *majorero* (the islanders)

Three authentic island accommodations

○ Hotel Rural Mahoh, Villaverde (►62)

○ Casa Isaítas, Pájara (►82)

○ Hotel Era de la Corte, Antigua (►82)

The island offers beach and water sports as well as wild views and traditional restaurants

Best host on the island

- Omar, the Argentine-born owner of the Cotillo Sunset Apartments (➤ 62)

Best shopping

- The Museo Artesanía in the Casa Santa María in Betancuria is the best one-stop souvenir and gift shop on the island. The shops in the airport departure lounge are remarkably good too

The wow factor

- The view of Risco del Paso beach from the roadside mirador to the north

The "I wish I'd discovered it earlier" award

- Isla de Lobos for its away-from-it-all feeling, especially for Corralejo holidaymakers (➤ 51–52)

Most ramshackle hamlet

- A dead heat between Cofete (➤ 98) and El Puertito, Isla de Lobos (➤ 51–52)

Scariest road

- Morro Jable to Cofete. The final part of the journey is a steep winding mountainside-hugging dirt road, which becomes almost single track (➤ 97–99)

Best walk

- Isla de Lobos, where you can pretend you're a desert island explorer (➤ 51–52)

Most controversial island project

- Montaña Tindaya Cube – a project to drill a cathedral-sized hole into the island's most sacred mountain (➤ 57)

Exhibits of traditional crafts in Centro Insular de Artesania at Betancuria (top). A distant view of the Isla de Lobos (bottom)

Finding Your Feet

First Two Hours

Arriving by air
- The **Aeropuerto de Fuerteventura** is 5km (3 miles) south of Puerto del Rosario on the east coast, tel: 928 860 500, www.aena.es.
- The major **car hire** companies have desks in the Arrivals Hall.
- There are currency exchange facilities, a café and basic shops, including a bookshop where you can buy island maps.

Getting to your resort from the airport
- **Taxis** are the quickest but most expensive option and leave from outside the airport building. Official prices are posted by the luggage carousel, at the airport information desk. Airport Taxis tel: 928 855 432.
- There is a direct **bus** service from the airport, just outside the terminal building, to Caleta de Fuste (No 3), Costa Calma (No 10) and Morro Jable (No 10). If you are staying in Corralejo or El Cotillo catch No 1 or 3 to Puerto del Rosario then take bus No 6 to Corralejo or No 7 to El Cotillo. (Bus No 8 links Corralejo to El Cotillo.)

Car hire at the airport
- Several major car hire companies have offices at the **airport**. Car hire is also **widely available** in the **main resorts** so unless you are staying somewhere remote you may have the option of travelling to your accommodation by bus or taxi then hiring a car when you get there (see opposite for more on car hire).

Arriving/Departing by sea
Tenerife and Gran Canaria
- **Passenger and car ferries** from Puerto del Rosario to Gran Canaria (Las Palmas), Morro Jable to Las Palmas, Morro Jable to Santa Cruz de Tenerife, Corralejo to Playa Blanca (Lanzarote), and Gran Tarajal/Puerto del Rosario to Las Palmas are operated by Naviera Armas shipping line (tel: 902 456 500, www.naviera-armas.com).

Lanzarote
- Passengers from Lanzarote (either Playa Blanca or Puerto del Carmen) arrive at Corralejo. Fred Olsen (tel: 902 100 107, www.fredolsen.es) and Naviera Armas (tel: 902 456 500) run a daily service every two hours from 7am (first boat from Playa Blanca) to 8pm (last return to Playa Blanca).

Morocco
- There are plans for a Naviera Armas ferry service between Fuerteventura and Tarfaya in Morocco, to commence early 2008. See their website www.naviera-armas.com for details.

Tourist information offices
- Most tourist office staff speak English and German and can issue **maps and information** in English and German.

Airport
- There is an office in the **Arrivals Hall**. Open: Mon–Sat 9–8, Sun 10–5 in winter, and Mon–Sat 9–7, Sun 11–4 in summer (tel: 928 860 604).

Resorts

- **Corralejo**. Playa Muelle Chico, Avenida Marítima 2. Open: Mon–Fri 8–3, Sat, Sun 9–3; 8–2 Jul, Aug and Sep (tel: 928 866 235, www.corralejo-grandesplayas.com). **Caleta de Fuste**, CC Castillo Centro, Calle Juan Ramón Soto Morales. Open: Mon–Fri 9–2 (tel: 928 163 286). **Jandía Playa/Morro Jable**. CC Cosmo Local 88. Open: Mon–Fri 8–3 (tel: 928 540 776). Morro Jable, on the beach just off the promenade there are three kiosks. One is open 10–1 and two are open 10–5.
- The **Patronato Insular de Turismo** (Island Tourist Board) has its offices at Almirante Lallermand, 1 in Puerto del Rosario. Open: Mon–Fri 8–3; 8–2 Jun–Sep (tel: 928 530 844).
- There are also tourist information kiosks at: **Antigua** Main square. Open: Mon–Fri 10–2 (tel: 928 163 286). **Betancuría**, next to the church. Open: Mon–Fri 10–2:30. **Gran Tarajal**, Avenida Paco Hierro, just off the main promenade. Open: Mon–Fri 10–2:30, Sat 9–1 (tel: 928 162 723).

Getting Around

Buses

- Buses are operated by **Tiadhe** (tel: 928 852 166, www.tiadhe.com) and are modern and comfortable. However, the service between resorts and places of interest is infrequent. Pick up a timetable from the nearest bus station or tourist office, or go online.

Taxis

- Taxis are usually white and have a green light on the top which when illuminated indicates that they are available for hire.
- For **local** journeys fares are **metered** (47–58c per km, min €2.68 (day-time, €3.21 (evening), but if travelling across municipal boundaries the meter does not apply and you must **agree a fare** in advance.
- Use the **regulated list of taxi fares** at the airport (see opposite) as a guide.
- You can usually hail a taxi on the street. The resorts and Puerto del Rosario have taxi ranks but at night book through your hotel.
- Taxi telephone numbers:
  Corralejo: 928 866 108, Morro Jable 928 541 257

Driving

- If you want to explore you need to hire a car (see below). On the whole driving is enjoyable with very **little traffic** and well-surfaced roads. The only downside is that this encourages **fast driving** so be wary of your own speed and that of the locals.
- **Take great care** when pulling off the road as the surface is nearly always raised 20cm (8in) or so above the ground level and you could easily damage the underneath of your vehicle. *Miradores* (lookout points) are usually provided in the mountains at particularly scenic spots so that you can pull over safely to enjoy the view.

Car hire

- Most **major international** car hire companies have offices at the airport.
- **Local companies** usually offer the best deals. If you want the security of a pre-booked car, however, you can use the services of a broker such as Holiday Autos (UK tel: 0870 400 4461) or visit www.holidayautos.co.uk or www.holidayautos.de.

- To **hire a car** you will need your passport, driver's licence and credit card. Keep these papers on you at all times, along with the car hire documents.
- If you intend driving off road, hire a **4WD/jeep** that the car hire company recommends for this purpose. These are available from all the main operators but book as far in advance as possible as they only have limited numbers. If you have an accident or damage the underside of any other vehicle while driving off road, your **insurance** will not cover this. Note that some operators threaten to levy a fine of around €120 (to cover the cost of wear and tear) if they see drivers take their ordinary saloon cars off road. You may wish to ask about this at time of hire or consult the small print in your contract.
- It's usually worth paying that bit extra for **air conditioning**.

Driving essentials
- Drive on the **right-hand** side of the road.
- **Seat belts** are compulsory for the driver and all passengers.
- The legal **alcohol** limit is 80mg alcohol per 100ml blood.
- **Speed limits** are 90kph (56mph) on the open road and 40kph (25mph) in urban areas unless otherwise indicated.
- Use your **horn** on blind bends in the mountains.
- **Fuel** is much cheaper than in northern Europe and on mainland Spain. Filling stations are few and far between in the mountains, so keep your tank topped up. Most, but not all, accept credit cards.
- **Theft** from cars is not a problem; nonetheless, lock valuable items in the boot.
- **Beware** that almost every town and village, no matter how small, has a one-way system. Be careful as they are not always well signposted – if every car in the street is parked facing towards you, you are probably going the wrong way!
- **Blue lines** indicate pay-and-display metered parking areas, yellow lines mean no parking.

Admission charges

The cost of admission for museums and places of interest mentioned in the text is indicated by the following categories:
Inexpensive = under €3   **Moderate** = €3–6   **Expensive** = over €6

Accommodation

The majority of hotels and apartments are booked by tour operators so independent travellers may experience some difficulty in finding places to stay. However, there is usually a surfeit of accommodation on the island so even in high season and holiday times there is always still a reasonable chance of getting something reasonable on spec.

- Timeshare touts do exist on Fuerteventura but are not yet a major problem. However, with the amount of new construction in the pipeline they are likely to increase in numbers. Be wary of anyone stopping you in the street or offering free excursions or prizes, as hard-sell tactics are often used to get your signature on a property deal. The golden rule is sign nothing without consulting your lawyer.

Hotels

- All hotels are officially graded from 1 to 5 stars, with most establishments rated as 3 stars or higher. In this category all bedrooms have a private bathroom.
- The hotels and apartments on the following pages have been selected because of their quality, special character or as being good value within their class or price range. Accommodation is more expensive during the peak season (late October to April). There is a second peak in late July and August when many Spanish families as well as northern Europeans are on holiday. The quietest months are May, June, early July, September and early October.

Apartments

- Apartments are graded from 1 to 3 keys, and even the simplest has a bedroom, bathroom, lounge, kitchenette and balcony. Bed linen, bath towels and maid service are usually included in the price; equipment such as TVs, kettles and toasters can usually be hired for an extra charge. Aparthotels are large apartment blocks with all the facilities of a hotel, such as a swimming pool, restaurant and evening entertainment.
- The majority of self-catering accommodation is pre-booked by package tourists but if you ask around in a resort you can usually find an apartment to let.

Casas rurales

- *Casa rurales* are village houses and farmsteads that have been con- verted into holiday cottages for rent. They are all small (accommodating a maximum of six people) and all are outside the resorts so you will definitely need a car. They are decorated in a rustic style (bare stone or wooden floors and rag rugs) and offer very good value, though not all have all mod cons, and certainly no air conditioning! If you crave a little more comfort, choose one of the island's three *hoteles rurales*, which accommodate more people, albeit still on a very small scale, and offer more facilities. Go to www.ecoturismocanarias.com/fuerteventura then click on Accommodations.

Prices

The symbols refer to the average cost of a double room or one-bedroom apartment in high season. In the case of larger hotels these are published "rack rates" and can usually be negotiated down.
€ under €60   €€ €60–90   €€€ €91–120   €€€€ over €120

Food and Drink

Most restaurants in Fuerteventura offer Canarian cuisine (➤ 18–21) together with steaks, seafood dishes and traditional Spanish favourites. Fresh fish is available all over the island.

What and where to eat

- Resorts such as Corralejo, Morro Jable, Jandía Playa and particularly Caleta de Fuste have a **full range of restaurants** offering English breakfasts, hamburgers, pizzas, wiener schnitzel, and other reminders of home, to their international clients.

> **Five popular tapas on Fuerteventura**
> *Albóndigas* (meatballs)
> *Croquetas* (croquettes), which may be filled with potato or cod
> *Gambas* (prawns)
> *Pimientos* (peppers), which may be stuffed with a variety of fillings
> *Pulpo* (octopus)

■ Many bars and some restaurants offer **tapas**, small portions of Spanish and Canarian food, which can either be starters, snacks or combined to act as a full meal.

Eating out – a practical guide
■ The traditional **mealtimes** are 1–4 for lunch and 8–11 for dinner, though many restaurants are open throughout the day to cater for the varying demands of locals and tourists.
■ Some restaurants offer a fixed-price *menú del día*, though this is the exception rather than the rule and is more likely to appear at lunchtime.
■ By law, **service** is included in the price, though there may be a nominal cover charge for items such as bread and olives or other snacks, which appear on the table unrequested. If you are happy with the service (see below) leave a tip of between five and ten per cent. In bars leave some small change on the counter.
■ Service is variable. In some local bars in particular standards of service may appear low (even unacceptably rude) to north Europeans while this is accepted as the norm locally.
■ **Booking** is rarely necessary except at the smartest or most popular restaurants (noted in the guide under regions). However, to avoid disappointment it may be worth making a reservation for Saturday dinner or Sunday lunch.

> **Five vegetarian dishes or tapas**
> *Papas arrugadas* with *mojo picón* (► 18)
> *Tortilla* (potato omelette)
> *Croquetas* (croquettes), which may be filled with potato or seafood
> *Pimientos* (peppers), which may be stuffed with a variety of fillings so enquire
> *Champiñónes* (mushrooms), usually stuffed with garlic and fried

■ **Prices**: With just a few exceptions, there is surprisingly little difference in prices when eating out. It is quite acceptable to order two starters and no main course, or a single starter for two people to share.
■ "**Children's menu**" generally means fast food or international food. If you want to avoid this, just ask for a smaller portion (*porción pequeña*) of an adult dish.

A guide to drinking
■ **Mineral water** is available everywhere. Ask for *agua sin gas* (still) or *agua con gas* (sparkling).

- **Coffee** is served as *café solo* (a small shot of strong black coffee, like an espresso) or *café con leche* (with milk). The latter is usually served with steamed milk and is similar to a cappuccino though some places may simply add warm, or even cold, milk. If you want an instant coffee, ask for a nescafé. A *baraquillo* is a shot of brandy in a black coffee and is popular after dinner.
- Small quantities of **wine** are produced in Fuerteventura though the most common Canary island wine in Fuerteventura is malvasia, either dry or sweet, from Lanzarote. Good-quality wines are imported from all over the Spanish mainland.
- The **local spirit** is *ron* (rum) and *ronmiel* (literally honey rum) is a popular liqueur.
- Many restaurants routinely serve a complimentary glass of sweet local liqueur at the end of a meal.

Prices
The symbols indicate what you should pay per person for a three-course meal, excluding drinks and service charge.
€ under €15   €€ €15–25   €€€ over €25

Shopping

Despite Spain's membership of the European Union (EU), the Canary Islands have retained their special status as a free trade zone, with minimal import duties and a low rate of value added tax (VAT) of 4.5 per cent. Many everyday and gift items, most notably alcohol, tobacco, perfume, jewellery and electronic goods, are considerably cheaper here than in many parts of mainland Europe. However, because the Canaries are not officially part of the EU, there are strict limits to the amount of goods that can be exported for personal use. The allowances to other EU countries are one litre of spirits, two litres of wine and either 200 cigarettes or 50 cigars.

Shopping areas
- The biggest **range** of shops is to be found in Corralejo and Jandía Playa, but still choice is limited. As well as Canarian crafts (see below), there are dozens of surf shops (usually very expensive); perfumeries and jewellers both offering duty-free prices; and electronics shops selling watches, cameras and high-tech goods. The latter are invariably run by Asian traders and prices are almost always negotiable.

Opening times
- Most shops are open Monday to Saturday from around 9:30/10–1:30 and 4:30/5–8. In Corralejo and Jandía Playa many shops open later, until around 10pm.
- The airport departure lounge has a surprisingly good choice of shops and good quality merchandise.

Canarian classics
- There are government-approved *artesanías* (craft shops) at Betancuria, El Molino de Antigua, the Ecomuseo de la Alcogida and at the airport. Everything on sale is handmade and there are no bargains.

- Locally produced goods include **basketry**, **embroidered lace**, **pottery** and *aloe vera* products.
- Favourite **foods** include *mojo* sauces, cheese and Canarian wines (usually from Lanzarote), Cuban-style cigars from La Palma.

Markets

- A general market for visitors tours the island every week. Goods on sale include **leatherwork**, **clothes**, **linens**, **lace**, **embroidery** and **ceramics**. Be prepared for a little bartering to get a decent price. The market is held from 9–1 at Corralejo on Monday and Friday, Caleta de Fuste on Saturday and Jandía Playa on Thursday.

Tattoo tradition

Although they probably do not realize it, the many **tattoo shops** in the resorts are following a centuries-old island tradition. It is thought that the original island inhabitants used *pintaderas* (wooden or pottery stamp blocks, carved with geometric patterns) to ornament their bodies. These are often on sale in the craft shops.

Five gifts made in Fuerteventura

- A Fuerteventura goat logo shirt/bag/other accessory
- A T-shirt with the island's famous podomorph (stylized footstep)
- Aloe vera products (but check they really are from Fuerteventura!)
- Handmade ethnic pottery
- A *pintadera* (see above)

Entertainment

Festivals and folklore

- **Fiestas** on the island are not as big or frequent as on the other popular Canary Islands but they still celebrate *Carnaval* (▶ 15–16), with the most colourful revelries in Corralejo and Puerto del Rosario.

Bars and clubs

- The busiest tourist **nightlife** is in Corralejo with the "music square" being the liveliest. Corralejo also has three good-quality nightspots. Caleta de Fuste and Jandía Playa also have a number of music bars. Locals will tell you that Puerto del Rosario has the best **nightclubs** on the island.

Water sports

- Conditions for **water sports**, particularly **windsurfing** and **kiteboarding**, are among the best in the world. This has attracted some of the finest training schools to both Corralejo and the Jandía beaches (▶ 12–13).
- **Surfing** is also very popular particularly around Corralejo and El Cotillo (▶ 13–14).
- **Scuba-diving** is a popular activity with many accredited schools (▶ 27).

Other sports

- There is a good **golf** course at Caleta de Fuste, which hosts the Canaries Spanish Open (▶ 84) and another 18-hole course at Jandía (▶ 106). Several hotels have **tennis** courts.

The North

Getting Your Bearings 44 – 45
In Four Days 46 – 47
Don't Miss 48 – 54
At Your Leisure 55 – 57
Where to… 58 – 64

Getting Your Bearings

Fuerteventura is often described as "a chip off the Sahara", with the coast of Africa just 100km (60 miles) northwest of Corralejo. And as you gaze out over the blinding dunes of Corralejo it seems a very apt description. Drive a little way inland and soft white sands change to jagged black rocks – *malpais* (volcanic debris) spilled from the dozens of volcanoes that were active here as recently as 8,000 years ago.

The island's only waymarked trail takes you on a lonely walk right into the heart of these "badlands", yet the north is also the busiest part of the island. All things are relative of course, and the biggest resort on Fuerteventura would hardly register a blip in Tenerife or Gran Canaria. However, if you have come to the island for peace and quiet, Corralejo should not be your first choice. It has wonderful beaches, a tremendous choice of places to eat, drink and make merry but while the old part retains its fishing village atmosphere, the new "strip" is modern and noisy.

For a taste of desert island bliss, slip quietly over to the Isla de Lobos. The unspoiled villages of Lajares and Villaverde are perfect country retreats and El Cotillo, with wonderful beaches

for all activities and ages, has a rustic, half-forgotten air, though major new developments may change all that. La Oliva is a quiet provincial seat with some intriguing historical and art attractions, while to the south Montaña Tindaya, the sacred mountain of the Guanches, provides a taster of the island's inland delights.

Punta c
Paso Chic

Playa de Te

Enjoy local churches or spend a day on Isla de Lobos

★ Don't Miss

1 Corralejo, Parque Natural de las Dunas de Corralejo ➤ 48
2 Isla de Lobos ➤ 51
3 La Oliva ➤ 53

At Your Leisure

4 El Cotillo ➤ 55
5 Lajares ➤ 55
6 Villaverde ➤ 56
7 Montaña Tindaya ➤ 57

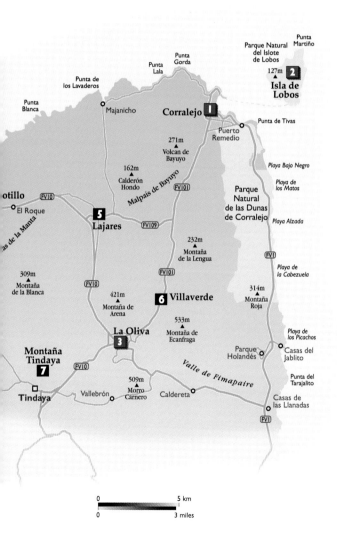

0   5 km

0   3 miles

The North in Four Days

Day One

Morning

Head out to the **❶ dunes of Corralejo** (➤ 50) to see one of the island's natural wonders. Cross the road and spend the morning at Flag Beach, indulge yourself with some water sports at Flag Beach Centre (➤ 64) and either have a snack lunch at the beach bar here or save yourself for lunch at Villaverde.

Afternoon

Drive to **❻ Villaverde** (➤ 56–57) and take your pick between its two excellent country restaurants, El Horno and the Hotel Rural Mahoh. Visit La Rosita museum and take a camel ride, then go underground at the Cueva del Llanos (➤ 56).

Day Two

Morning

Drive to **❸ La Oliva** (➤ 53–54) and visit the Centro de Arte Canario. Leave your car by the museum, visit the church (decorated ceiling, above), the Casa de los Coroneles and the nearby Casa del Capellán (➤ 54). Return to your car and visit the tiny Museo del Grano La Cilla (➤ 54) just around the corner. Get back on the main road and drive to **❹ El Cotillo** (➤ 55) for lunch at El Veril, Azzuro or Torino's beach bar (➤ 59–60).

Afternoon

Spend the afternoon on the family-friendly Lagos lagoon beaches or catch a wave at the magnificent wild beaches to the south of town. Visit the beautifully restored Torre del Tostón (➤ 55) overlooking the new port and watch the sunset here. Finish your day with a meal at El Veril or Azzuro (➤ 59–60).

Day Three

Get down to the port at Corralejo early to watch the comings and goings (above and right), have breakfast at La Olá café (➤ 58–59), then catch the 10am ferry to visit the **2 Isla de Lobos** (➤ 51–52) for a day of desert island exploring and/or sunbathing. Return at either 4pm or 6pm and spend the rest of the evening shopping, bar-hopping and dining in Corralejo.

Day Four

Morning

Strap on your walking shoes, drive to Lajares and explore the north's volcanic landscape by taking the Sendero de Bayuyo (➤ 142). Return to **5 Lajares** (➤ 55–56), browse at the craft stalls, and either have a simple lunch at El Arco (➤ 60) or head to El Cotillo (below) for lunch at El Veril or Azzuro (➤ 59).

Afternoon

If you can drag yourself away from El Cotillo's beaches, drive towards La Oliva then head south to see the magical **7 Montaña Tindaya** (➤ 57). From here it's a very pleasant drive along the FV10 through La Matilla and Tetir until you reach the outskirts of Puerto del Rosario. Follow the signs back to Corralejo, which is 33km (20 miles) north.

Corralejo

The biggest resort on the island, Corralejo has a loyal following, particularly among British visitors. The town divides neatly into "old port" and "new resort" with the dividing line being the pedestrianised zone. Just beyond this zone is the original fishing harbour, now a busy port where the Lanzarote and Lobos ferries, big-game fishing yachts and sleek catamarans jostle for space alongside traditional fishing boats.

The old part of town, particularly around the pedestrianised zone, is a picturesque area of small alleys and squares, most of which lead onto the seafront promenade, which is lined with attractive restaurants and bars. The epicentre of nocturnal activities is "Music Square", a tiny quadrangle hemmed in by restaurants with waiters touting for trade and a small stage where musicians serenade diners. To find the most authentic Spanish and local bars and restaurants, and some quaint little shops, just go a block or two further on towards the port. On Calle La Ballena it's hard to go wrong.

The modern part of town lies to either side of Avenida Nuestra Señora del Carmen, aka "The Strip". The Avenida is not unattractive and has several shopping centres, but don't expect to buy your designer gear here. However, if you want amusement arcades, cheap shops and eateries, as well as several Irish bars, then you should be happy (and well oiled) here.

Fly a kite on Corralejo's wide, open beaches and look out for sand sculptures on the town beach

Baku

The north's main visitor attraction began life as a water park with eight flumes and slides. It has now grown to include two other major attractions – Animal Experience, with a petting zoo, sea lion and parrot shows (visitors can enter the water with the sea lions at an extra charge if they book in advance), and El Hotel del Terror, a haunted house with real actors. Other family-oriented activities include an enchanted castle, a zipwire, paintballing, a rock-climbing wall, mini-golf, ten-pin bowling and bingo. There is a Brazilian restaurant with shows every Friday evening and a market is held every Monday and Friday morning with African and Canarian handicrafts.

Explore Corralejo's architecture, eateries and nightlife

Beaches

The town harbour beach is the easy option, right in the centre, although it can get crowded. Look out for some very artistic and sophisticated sand sculptures here and do throw a coin or two in the artist's hat, particularly if you take a photograph. Moving east from the harbour a narrow beach runs almost all the way along the front. Playa Galera, in front of the Corralejo Beach hotel, is a nice stretch. The best beaches lie 500m (550 yards) or so east of here and stretch for around 7km (4 miles). You can easily walk from the newer part of town but if you are staying near the port and/or you are driving, then it is "just around the corner" from the main road into Corralejo (like most Spanish towns it has an unforgiving one-way system!).

Flag Beach is the main section and the next stretch along, by the two large Riu hotels, is known as Glass Beach.

Windsurfers and kitesurfers will head to Flag Beach or Glass Beach but there are excellent surfing "beaches" (with no sand) heading west from the Bristol Playas apartments. Whichever beach you choose, directly across the water you will enjoy great views of Isla de Lobos and Lanzarote.

Parque Natural de las Dunas de Corralejo

Corralejo's white sand dunes cover an area of around 27sq km (10 square miles). This area was declared a national park in 1982, too late to stop the two hotels that were already built, but it did prevent further attempts to exploit this otherwise pristine natural landscape.

Escape to the dunes of the pristine Parque Natural de las Dunas de Corralejo

Walk for ten minutes off the road, out of sight and sound of traffic and hotels, and you could imagine yourself in a Lawrence of Arabia world. The only creatures you will meet are a handful of goats and the occasional naturist.

TAKING A BREAK

If you're after a coffee or food, the Antiguo Café del Puerto (➤ 58) is an all-day option.

➕ 163 E5

Baku Water Park
➕ 168 A1 ✉ Avenida Nuestra Señora del Carmen ☎ 928 867 227 🕐 Daily 10–5 (later in season) 💷 Expensive

---

CORRALEJO: INSIDE INFO

Top tip If you are around during the second weekend in October, don't miss the **Kite Festival** held by the dunes.

One to miss The **town beach** is not always as clean as it might be.

Hidden gem On the Avenida Fuerteventura (the main road to the beaches and dunes) keep your eyes peeled for the **Villa Tabaiba Galeria de Arte** (it's No 139 next to an apartment complex with an Irish pub). It is privately owned and open at irregular times (afternoons are the best bet), but even if there's no admission it's well worth stopping to peer into the garden to view the owner's eccentric collection of artworks heavily influenced by Salvador Dalí and Joan Miró.

Must see Isla de Lobos (➤ 51–52)

2 Isla de Lobos

It seems everything on the Isla de Lobos qualifies itself by a diminutive; *las lagunitas*, the little lagoons; *los hornitos*, the little volcanoes; El Puertito, the (ramshackle) little port. We would add to that by saying that this is the best little day trip that you can make. The absence of tourist development means that you can see an almost pristine island in its original state.

Isla de Lobos measures 4.4sq km (1.7 square miles) and you can walk right around the perimeter in less than two hours. Our featured walk (➤ 138–141) of around three hours, takes you to all the island's places of interest and is highly recommended. The island name, literally "island of wolves", is derived from a colony of seals (*lobos marineros*), in fact monk seals, which once lived here but have long since disappeared. It is recorded that the explorer and conquistador Gadifer de la Salle (number two to Jean de Béthencourt, ➤ 9–11) dropped anchor here in 1402 and he and his men were only saved from starving by eating seal meat. Béthencourt built a hermitage on the island and in the following centuries Lobos was used as a pirate and slave-trading base. Today the only permanent residents are António, the ex-lighthouse keeper, now island restaurateur, his family and a few friends who inhabit the dilapidated little hamlet of El Puertito. The lighthouse still functions but is now fully automated.

Isla de Lobos is just a few minutes across the water

Getting here

There are three boats that run daily to the island from Corralejo. *Isla de Lobos* is the regular service departing at 10:15 and 11:45am, returning at noon and 4:15pm. The *Celia Cruz* glass-bottomed catamaran (mob: 646 531 068, www.fuerteventura.net/celiacruz departs at 9:45am and returns at

2:30pm and 6pm (Oct–May 5:15pm). The *El Majorero* departs at 10 and noon and returns at 12:30pm and 4pm. If you intend to walk, sunbathe and eat in the restaurant here, choose the *Celia Cruz* as it gives you more time. The *Celia Cruz* also offers a daily one-hour cruise around the island. Pick up a flyer from their kiosk on the quay at Corralejo for departure times.

Two boats run to Isla de Lobos, including a glass-bottomed catamaran

Getting about

It couldn't be easier. Signposts show you the way as soon as you disembark. The island's only settlement, El Puertito, is a seven-minute walk to the right; the beautiful beach of Playa la Concha (aka Playa de la Calera) lies six minutes to the left. Walkers and explorers will be delighted to find that a waymarked trail goes right around the island, with the furthest point being the Faro (lighthouse) de Lobos, a 48-minute walk due north.

TAKING A BREAK

If you intend to eat at the island restaurant you MUST make a reservation as soon as you land (➤ 141 for more details).

🞥 163 E5

ISLA DE LOBOS: INSIDE INFO

One to miss Avoid visiting on very **windy days**.

Hidden gem El Puertito springs surprisingly to life around lunchtime. The smell of fresh fish wafts from **Antonio's** rustic restaurant, the little bay in front of here is ideal for swimming, a jet ski is sometimes available for rides, and divers also turn up here.

③ La Oliva

Despite being the adminis-
trative centre of the north,
La Oliva is no more than a
large village and often has
the appearance of a ghost
town. Nonetheless, it has an
interesting history and a
number of unusual sights.

La Oliva has always been a seat of
power on Fuerteventura. The
Guanche king Guize (► 9–10) once
ruled his northern territory from
here, and after the conquest it was
one of the first towns to be settled by
the Europeans.

   The Iglesia de Nuestra Señora de la Candelaria, built in
1711, has three naves, but its most striking feature is its
black lava bell tower. Look inside to see its wine-glass-
shaped pulpit and side altar decorated in matching
patterns and its painting of Christ in Majesty (1732).

Casa de los Coroneles

When the island rulers decamped to Lanzarote in 1709, the
newly established military governor of the island (*El Coronel*, or
the Colonel) chose La Oliva as his headquarters. The seat of
power was the grandiose Casa de los Coroneles, a large
castellated colonial-style house dating back to 1650. It used to
be said, quite erroneously, that there was a door and window for
every day of the year and it is thought that the saying probably
reflected the jealous unpopularity of the Colonel's regime. This
came to an end in 1859 and thereafter the famous old house
begdan a long slow decline into dereliction. After decades of
promises of renewal had come and gone, restoration was
completed and the Casa de Coroneles reopened in 2006 as an
art gallery and cultural centre (open Tue–Sat 10–6).

The Nuestra
Señora de la
Candelaria
church is well
worth a visit

Centro de Arte Canario
(CAC)

This cool contemporary space
devoted to Canarian art,
complete with soothing
ambient New Age music,
has wide-ranging appeal.
The entrance is via a large
sculpture and cactus garden
with several interesting and
witty pieces alluding to the
island's flora, fauna and

ancient history. Its centrepiece is the Casa Mané, a restored mid-19th-century house, including six paintings by Lanzarote guru César Manrique (➤ 108).

Museo del Grano La Cilla

A *cilla* is a storehouse for grain that belongs to the church, and this example dates from 1819. It was used to house wheat, barley, rye, pulses and some fruit. Today it is home to a small exhibition of photographs and agricultural implements that show how farming was done manually with the aid of donkeys and camels until the 1940s.

TAKING A BREAK

La Oliva is short of good cafés or restaurants but try Casa Malpey on the El Cotillo Road (➤ 60).

Visit the Centro de Arte Canario (top) and see the artefacts at the Museo del Grano La Cilla

➕ 163 D3

Centro de Arte Canario (CAC)
➕ 163 D3 ✉ Calle Salvador Manrique de Lara (opposite Casa de los Coroneles) ☎ 928 851 128, www.centrodeartecnario.com 🕐 Mon–Sat 10:30–2 💷 Moderate

Museo del Grano La Cilla
➕ 163 D3 ✉ Carretera El Cotillo ☎ 928 868 729 🕐 Tue–Fri, Sun 9:30–5:30 💷 Inexpensive

---

LA OLIVA: INSIDE INFO

Must see The village springs to life on 2 February for the four-day **fiesta of Nuestra Señora de la Candelaria**.

Hidden gem The **Casa del Capellán** (House of the Chaplain) stands boarded up in a field of dilapidated smallholding buildings, around 100m (110 yards) to the right of the road that leads to the Casa de los Coroneles. Despite its run-down appearance, the fine carvings around the door of this modest single-storey 200-year-old house are reminiscent of the famous portal at the church at Pájara (➤ 78), often described as "Aztec" influenced.

Top tip Illuminate the church by putting €1 in the slot.

At Your Leisure

4 El Cotillo

At first sight it might seem there's little to detain you here, but persevere and you'll find some of the most attractive beaches and two of the best restaurants (➤ 59) on the island. El Cotillo is also a great place to watch the sunset. Historical interest is provided by the restored **Fortaleza/ Torre del Tostón** (Tostón Tower), constructed in 1740 to deter English, Moorish and Arab pirates. Today it is home to a tourist office – climb the stairs for fine views over the *puerto nuevo* (new harbour) with its little fishing boats sheltering behind a huge volcanic rock. The dramatic high-sided jet-black *puerto viejo* (old harbour), occupying the next cove along, is usually empty of boats.

Head north of El Cotillo for magnificent wild windswept surfing beaches; to the south follow the signs for Playas Lagos (lagoon beaches), gorgeous little white-sand family-friendly coves sheltered from the breakers by volcanic reefs.

➕ 162 C4

Fortaleza/Torre del Tostón
✉ El Tostón ⏰ Daily 9–4, Oct–Jun; 9–3, Jul–Sep; closed public holidays 💶 Moderate

5 Lajares

This small roadside village has long been a popular stopping point for surfers en route to El Cotillo, and in recent years it has also attracted many foreign property buyers. The presence of both groups is reflected in a spate of good cafés, restaurants

and surf shops. Lajares is also known for its long-established School of Embroidery, nowadays incorporated into an *artesanía* (handicrafts) shop (➤ 63). There are two fine examples of restored windmills near the church

Try the restaurants at El Cotillo

Three best Canarian meals
• **Hotel Rural Mahoh**, Villaverde (➤ 60)
• **El Horno**, Villaverde (➤ 60)
• **El Veril**, El Cotillo (➤ 59–60)

The power of the sea

The restaurant El Veril in El Cotillo's old harbour features the work of island photographer Jo Hammer. Among his most powerful images are those of recent storms when the waves reached over 10m (32 feet) high and gave El Cotillo a terrible battering. Postcard-sized prints are on sale and make a good souvenir.

The Cueva Villaverde

The Cueva Villaverde is a cave formed by volcanic gases and lava, and measures some 190m long. It was used as a Guanche dwelling place and only discovered in 1979. There are long-term plans to open it up to the public but until then there is a small exhibition in the Centro Molino, La Antigua (➤ 83). Finds from the cave are on show in the Museo Arqueológico in Betancuría (➤ 72).

to the south of Lajares and the village is also the starting point for the Sendero de Bayuyo footpath (➤ 142).

✚ 163 D4

6 Villaverde

Villaverde is one of the best-preserved villages on the island. Perhaps the villagers are following the lead of the exemplary Hotel Rural Mahoh (➤ 60), which stands at the southern end of Villaverde and is worth a visit for its architecture and sculpture garden alone. The equally neat and tidy black-and-white stone farm buildings of La Rosita mark the northern entrance to the village. In the 1920s this was a tobacco and maize farm and, as the friendly owner will tell you, she was born, in fairly primitive conditions, in the front room of what is now a beautifully restored museum. Outside you can see where the maize is, where tobacco was grown, a cactus garden

Atlantis and ancient Egypt

Given the dramatic volcanic geology of the Canary Islands and their proximity to North Africa perhaps it is no surprise that they have long been associated with the myth of Atlantis and theories on Egyptology and links from there to extraterrestrials. Island photographer Jo Hammer has studied Mount Tindaya for many years and believes these links all come together here. Visit his site www.atlantura.com for details.

You can watch the intricacies of lace-making in Lajares, or (below) admire the views of Montaña Colorada

✚ 163 D4

La Rosita
✉ Carretera General La Oliva–Corralejo
km 6.7 ☎ 928 175 325 🕐 Mon–Fri
10–5, Sat 10–3 💷 Moderate

Cueva del Llano
☎ 928 175 928 🕐 Tue–Sat; tours
every 30 minutes from 10:15–12:45 and
2:45–5:15 💷 Moderate

Walk to the summit of Montaña Tindaya for
spectacular views

7 Montaña Tindaya

The original island dwellers regarded this
mountain as sacred and came up here to
worship their Supreme Deity, offering
young goats as sacrifices. Their legacy is a number of inscriptions and
rock carvings, only discovered as recently as 1978, on and around the
summit of the mountain at 401m (1,315 feet). The most famous are
over 100 feet-shaped carvings known as podomorphs. As these are on
the side of the mountain facing Mount Teide on Tenerife, which in
Guanche times erupted frequently and was considered as the abode of
the devil, so they are thought to have been carved to keep away evil
spirits. All the other rock carvings also face this way.

It takes just under two hours to reach the summit and on a clear day
there are stunning views right across to Mount Teide. It is a strenuous
climb, however, not suitable for inexperienced walkers and dangerous in
wet or windy weather. Because of its sensitive nature you are required
to have a permit, which in nearly all cases is issued on demand.
Enquire at the Medio Ambiente (Environment Office) in Puerto del
Rosario, Calle Primerode Mayo, 39; tel: 928 862 363.

Where to...
Eat and Drink

Prices
Expect to pay for a three-course meal for one, excluding drinks and service
€ under €15   €€ €15–25   €€€ over €25

CORRALEJO

Ambaradam €
Set on a quiet side street just off the top end of "The Strip", this Italian-owned and run café is a stylish, relaxed oasis in this part of town, perfect for a snack or full meal after visiting the market or the Baku amusement park. They specialise in breakfasts, sweet and savoury pancakes (no less than 47 kinds) and bruschetta (14 different types). Attentive friendly young staff and Italian football on TV.

➕ 168 B3 ⊠ Centro Commercial Cactus ☎ 696 996 207
🕐 Mon–Sat 8–1:30

Antiguo Café del Puerto €€
This is the sort of place you will be welcome at any time of day or night, whether you want a *café con leche* (coffee with milk) or a beer while watching the boats on the seafront, or to make yourself a meal up from the good choice of tasty tapas in its attractive pastel-washed dining room. The staff are friendly and obliging.

➕ 163 E5 ⊠ Calle La Ballena ☎ 928 535 844 🕐 Thu–Tue
11am–1am

Bodeguita El Andaluz €€
Manolo, the chef, is from Córdoba, and his menu is, like the restaurant itself, comprehensive but comfortably small. After the tasty home-made bread and oil tuck into a starter of garlic prawns, or avocado, mozzarella and tomato, or perhaps baby lettuce with roasted garlic. A speciality from Córdoba is the rich gazpacho-like *salmorejo* soup. Meat dishes – superior quality steaks, chicken, pork fillet and kebab – come with a choice of green pepper, herb butter or creamy mushroom sauce, and there is always a fresh fish of the day. No credit cards taken.

➕ 163 E5 ⊠ Calle La Ballena 5 ☎ 676 705 878 🕐 Thu–Tue
7pm–11pm

Caracoles €€
Sylvia and Carlos are well known to Corralejo regulars for their authentic Spanish/Canarian cooking and their latest venture, serving up some of the best tapas in town. An attractive little bar set in a narrow alleyway just off Music Square, it is unlikely to disappoint. Special offers such as six tapas and a bottle of wine for a set price makes the choosing less of a chore for confused visitors who would like a taste of everything.

➕ 163 E5 ⊠ Just off Music Square
🕐 Tue–Sun 7–11pm (closed last Sun of month)

Factoria €–€€
Set right on the seafront, but just away from the main hubbub, this cheerful little pizzeria is one of the friendliest places in Corralejo. They do steaks and fish but specialise in pizzas (try something different such as the Felipin with broccoli, bacon and salmon). The perfect dining choice for young families.

➕ 163 E5 ⊠ Avenida Marítima
☎ 928 535 726 🕐 Daily
10:30am–11pm

La Olá €
This attractive modern café attached to a bakery is just a stone's throw from

the port. They do excellent breakfasts – try the *desayuno español* (Spanish breakfast), which includes toasted bread drizzled in olive oil, rubbed with tomato and topped with *jamón serrano* (cured ham). Despite being locals, they specialise in German pastries, cakes and cheesecake, and their iced coffee *frappé* is delicious.

The service is friendly and fast, and there are comfy cane chairs; sit inside or out.

➕ 163 E5 ⌖ Paseo Marítimo Bristol, Muelle Grande ☎ 928 535 304 ◷ Wed–Mon 7.30am–8pm

Los Pepes €€

This has been one of Corralejo's favourite restaurants for several years and though it changed hands in 2007 it is still run by a dedicated husband-and-wife-team with more than 20 years experience in the kitchen. Alongside old favourites such as garlic prawns, pepper steak, and Thai fish cakes are more creative dishes, such as grilled Halloumi salad with nectarines;

griddled aubergines, stuffed with ricotta, garnished with feta and spring onions; Portuguese chicken and chorizo cooked in a cider and cream sauce; Galantine of chicken, stuffed with crab and tarragon mousse and served with a peanut sauce. The mouthwatering desserts are works of art.

➕ 163 E5 ⌖ Calle La Ballena ☎ 928 537 276, www.los-pepes.com ◷ Tue–Sun 6–11pm

Rogues Gallery

The accent is firmly on rock and blues at this friendly British-run music bar. The volume always permits conversation, however, and there is no TV. Live music is performed by a guitarist every Saturday night.

➕ 163 E5 ⌖ Calle La Ballena 3 ◷ Tue–Sun 10–1, 5–late

EL COTILLO

Aguayre €

This trendy modern bar overlooking the new port is the ideal place to catch

the famous El Cotillo sunset with a beer, smoothie, milkshake or *chai latte* in your hand. There's even a couple of hammocks in which to chill out. Gourmet sandwiches and international snacks such as chilli and burritos are served throughout the day.

➕ 162 C4 ⌖ Puerto Nuevo ◷ Daily 9:30–9

Azzurro €€

Roberto, the friendly Italian co-owner/chef, serves possibly the best Italian food on the island alongside a broad range of Canarian dishes and a good vegetarian menu. The paella and the *scoglio* (seafood) *tagliatelle* with mushrooms and prawns in a parmesan nest are highly recommended. Relax in the cosy traditional stone interior or on the terrace, watching the sunset alongside a mixed crowd of diners. There is live music every Friday at sunset. Azzurro provides excellent service and superb house wines.

➕ 162 C4 ⌖ Urb. Los Lagos 1,

Carretera al Faro ☎ 928 175 360 ◷ Tue–Sun 12:30–10:30

Torino €–€€

This friendly little beach bar next to the lagoon beaches serves a good range of snacks and full meals and is the ideal place to eat with warm sand between your toes. The garlic prawns are wonderful and the paella is good, but give the cheese and tomato salad a miss.

➕ 162 C4 ⌖ Playa Lagos ◷ Daily 10–5

El Veril €€

Unassuming from the front, the interior of this splendidly restored old house is one of the nicest places on the island to enjoy first-class Spanish and new wave Canarian cooking. The chef is Basque, and fish, meat and vegetarian dishes reflect the craft, style and top-class reputation of his home region. El Veril also has a large roof terrace overlooking the old harbour.

➕ 162 C4 ⌖ Muelle de los Pescadores ☎ 928 538 780,

www.restauranteelveril.com

🕑 Tue–Sat 6pm–midnight, Sun 1–4, 7–midnight

LAJARES

El Arco €

This friendly and very well run roadside café is the perfect place for a simple sandwich or more substantial snack when you want to sit with the locals and ex-pats and eat without fuss. El Arco offers excellent value *bocadillos* – especially recommended is the *lomo especial* with pork, *alioli* (whisked oil and garlic), salad, egg and cheese – and *platos combinados* (combined dishes).

➕ 163 D4 ⌧ Carretera Lajares-El Cotillo 🕾 928 868 071 🕑 Mon–Fri 9am–11pm, Sat 9–5

Mirando Al Sur €€

If you love your juicy steaks and grills you will love this Argentine-style *parrillada* (grill restaurant), which serves the tastiest and biggest chunks of meat on the island.

Beefsteaks come in all cuts and sauces plus there's rolled beef, Creole *chorizo*, *morcilla* (black pudding sausage), pork steaks, veal, rabbit and chicken cooked over a large open barbecue. There is a smaller branch, with equally tasty food, at Corralejo.

Lajares: ➕ 163 D4 ⌧ Calle La Laguna 🕾 928 536 287 🕑 Mon, Wed–Sun 1–11

Corralejo: ➕ 163 E5 ⌧ Calle Juan Sebastian Elcano, 5 🕾 928 536 287 🕑 Daily 1–4, 6:30–11:30

El Point €

This popular surfers' bar and café just off the beaten track serves juices, milkshakes, special teas, healthy snacks and meals, including vegetarian dishes and home-made desserts. Regular live (mostly world) music and DJs.

➕ 163 D4 ⌧ Calle La Laguna opposite the football stadium (behind Miranda Al Sur restaurant) 🕾 928 875 158, www.enesenciaelpoint.com 🕑 Tue–Sun 11–11

LA OLIVA

Casa Malpey €€

If you're in La Oliva at lunchtime and you're happy with typical Canarian cooking in surroundings to match, then opt for this restaurant with its simple menu. Ask the friendly owner which fish she recommends and go with that.

➕ 163 D3 ⌧ Calle La Orilla 67 (Carretera La Oliva-El Corillo) 🕾 928 888 060 🕑 Tue–Sun 1–11

VILLAVERDE

El Horno €€

The large barbecue at the entrance to this attractive rustic restaurant tells you that the speciality of the house is grilled meats. Start with aubergine with cheese and palm honey then perhaps *cochinillo* (suckling pig) or kid. Finish with fig or *gofio* ice cream. Lots of greenery and traditional Canarian music.

➕ 163 D4 ⌧ Carretera General Villaverde-La Oliva, 191

🕾 928 868 671, 629 382 304 🕑 Tue–Sat 12:30pm–11pm, Sun 12:30pm–4:30pm

Hotel Rural Mahoh €€

Choose from one of the most interesting Canarian menus on the island while relaxing in one of its most charming settings.

Start with delicious croquettes, stuffed peppers or baby squid with *mojo verde*; for mains try *vieja* (parrot fish) or goat, and finish with *leche frita* or fig ice cream smothered in mouth-watering warm chocolate sauce.

The daily *menú de la casa* (house special) is excellent value and on Sundays there are several roast specials on the blackboard. It is a very romantic setting by night and there is always excellent service.

➕ 163 D4 ⌧ Sitio de Juan Bello, Carretera Villaverde-La Oliva 🕾 928 868 050, www.mahoh.com 🕑 Daily 1–midnight

Where to...
Stay

Prices
Expect to pay per double room, per night
€ under €60 €€ €60–90 €€€ €91–120 €€€€ over €120

Note that many of the larger hotels and apartments in Corralejo are block booked by big tour operators.

CORRALEJO

Atlantis Bahía Real €€€€
If your idea of a holiday is pampered luxury, then this 5-star 250-room grand hotel in Moorish-style right on the beachfront, just out of town, is ideal. All rooms enjoy magnificent sea views, there are three gourmet restaurants to eat your way through and the largest and best-equipped spa on the island, with a Turkish Bath, an ice fountain, a shower temple, a large open-air jacuzzi, a spinning room and just about any treatment you could wish for.
➕ 163 E5 ⬜ Avenida Grandes Playas ☎ 928 536 444, www.atlantisbahiareal.com

Brisamar €
The popular Brisamar aparthotel offers spacious and comfortable one- or two-bedroom apartments with a terrace at a very reasonable price. The hotel features saltwater swimming pools (including one for children), two tennis courts and a playground.
➕ 163 E5 ⬜ Avenida Nuestra Señora del Carmen ☎ 928 866 525

Corralejo Beach €
One of the town's original and favourite accommodations, the Corralejo Beach, fully renovated in 2007, enjoys a good beachfront location right in the centre of the resort. It includes 156 studios and apartments, with basic but functional furnishings, many with views towards Lanzarote and Isla de Lobos. Facilities include a sauna, solarium and a swimming pool. It also has its own disco pub.
➕ 163 E5 ⬜ Avenida Nuestra Señora del Carmen 3 ☎ 928 866 315, www.corralejobeach.com

Los Delfines €
This simple, white, two-storey apartment complex is rated 3-keys and is a five-minute walk from the beach. The apartments are attractively arranged around the pool area and each has its own terrace or balcony. Facilities include a buffet restaurant and squash courts.
➕ 163 E5 ⬜ Calle El Pozo 3 ☎ 928 535 153, www.apartamentoslosdelfines.com

Hesperia Bristol Playa €€€
This attractive 3-keys aparthotel is situated on the seafront near the port and comprises 184 low-rise units in landscaped gardens. Apartments are well equipped and facilities include three outdoor swimming pools, tennis courts and garden bar.
➕ 163 E5 ⬜ Urbanización Lago de Bristol 1 ☎ 928 867 020, www.hesperia-bristolplaya.com

La Posada €
This comfortable, modern three-storey 34-room hotel is set in the pedestrianised part of town just two minutes from the port. However, while it is quiet during the day, it is very noisy from 4pm to 8pm due to the large children's playground in front of it. The staff and owners are

very friendly and obliging. Good breakfast. There's also a roof terrace. Excellent value.

➕ 163 E5 ✉ Calle María Santana Figueroa ☎ 928 867 344

Riu Palace Tres Islas €€€€

If location is your priority, the luxurious 4-star Tres Islas is one of the best options, located by magnificent white beaches right next to the dunes. It has two large swimming pools set in beautiful oasis-like grounds. The three isles referred to in the hotel's name are Lanzarote and Lobos (there are wonderful views of them just across the water) and Fuerteventura itself.

➕ 163 E5 ✉ Avenida Grandes Playas ☎ 928 535 700, www.riu.com

VILLAVERDE

Hotel Rural Mahoh €€

The Mahoh is an old country house built from volcanic stone and wood and dates from the 19th century. It has nine bedrooms with stone floors,

all furnished with antiques, four of them with four-poster beds, and all exuding a rustic and romantic feel. Within its manicured grounds there is a swimming pool, a multi-purpose sports area with tennis and horse-riding stables. Its restaurant (▶ 60) is one of the best on the island so *media pensión* (half board) is recommended. Breakfast is included in the price.

➕ 163 D4 ✉ Sitio de Juan Bello, Carretera Villaverde-La Oliva ☎ 928 868 050, www.mahoh.com

EL COTILLO

Casa Tile €€

Set 2km (1 mile) inland from El Cotillo this mid-19th-century country house is a perfect holiday hideaway for up to four people. The house has been in the same family for more than 150 years and has been recently sympathetically renovated and restored to retain its character. The living area, bathroom and bedrooms are separated from the kitchen and dining area by an open

courtyard and there is a small (3m x 4m/10 feet x 13 feet) pool. Other facilities include a TV, washing machine and barbecue. Minimum stay during mid and high season is one week.

➕ 162 C4 ✉ El Roque 🔒 From the UK call Secret Destinations, 0845 612 9000, www.secretdestinations.com or visit www.ecoturismocanarias.com

Cotillo Sunset Apartments €–€€

Right on the beach and a five-minute walk from the beautiful Lagos coves, this smart little modern complex comprises 32 two-storey studios. Each is attractively furnished and has well-equipped kitchens, including a microwave oven and toaster. All have a balcony/terrace with patio furniture. There is a 12m x 6m (40 feet x 20 feet) pool, a children's paddling pool and a heated outdoor jacuzzi. Snacks and delivered meals are provided by the El Veril restaurant (▶ 59). Best of all, the ever-helpful manager, Omar, is the perfect host.

➕ 162 C4 ✉ Avenida de los Dos

Lagos ☎ 928 175 065; UK guests can book through Secret Destinations, 0845 612 9000, www.secretdestinations.com, or visit www.cotillosunset.com

LAJARES

El Patio de Lajares €€€

This charming, stylish German-run "restaurant with rooms" is entered via a traditional-style patio and has six comfortable and spacious air-conditioned rooms in modern-traditional style and furnished to a high standard. Each has a terrace, satellite TV (English channels), mini bar, and a luxurious bathroom including bathrobes. There's a swimming pool, and wellness facilities include a Japanese reflexology foot bath, a small lava sand and mineral spa, a fitness centre and aloe vera treatments. The restaurant is highly recommended.

➕ 163 D4 ✉ Calle la Cerca 9, Lajares ☎ 650 134 030, www.patio-lajares.com

Where to...
Shop

Shopping in the north of the island is concentrated on the *centros comerciales* (shopping centres) and main street of Corralejo. There are very few shops elsewhere in this region.

CORRALEJO

The resort's "high street", Avenida Nuestra Señora del Carmen (also known as The Strip), and the many shopping centres that lead off here feature scores of fashion clothes shops. Surf wear is predominant and there are at least a dozen *bona fide* surf shops here too, although they are quite pricey. After a while, to the uninitiated at least, these all blur together, though the stylish Fuerte goat logo clothing at New Territory Fuerteventura is symbolic of the island.

International retail names sell at similar prices to northern Europe, but for something a bit different look in the bohemian Las Gatas with its Gaudi-like entrance. Another unusual shop along The Strip is the Panadería de Don Juan at number 20. This old-fashioned, long-established bakery is ideal if you're self catering, and they have a small cafe attached too.

Just off the Avenida, on the corner of Calle Lepanto and Calle Isaac Peral, World Natural Cotton has a good selection of reasonably priced linen and natural cotton wear, aimed at women in their mid-20s upwards. There are more pure cotton and linen clothes at Pachamama, which also specializes in aloe vera products. They have branches on The Strip and in Calle La Milagrosa.

For perfumes and cosmetics, Riu Parfum at the top of the Avenida has the best selection in town.

There are some pleasant little individual outlets dotted around the harbour. Mystic, on the corner of Calle Maria Santana Figueroa and Calle Isla de Lobos, is probably the best of

Corralejo's many "world shops". They feature aloe vera products, Haitian art, some intriguing large wooden sculptures and objets d'art, stylish silk clothes, ethnic jewellery and accessories. For more of the latter, try Arco Iris just around the corner.

Corralejo's market (▶ 42) takes place every Monday and Friday 9am to 1pm at Baku on Avenida Nuestra Señora del Carmen and is a good place to go if you enjoy haggling for African-style goods.

VILLAVERDE

The Casa Marcos, on the main road, is geared up for coach parties and resembles a mini-village. It has a good range of wines, cheeses, preserves, pottery and souvenirs. Food items and home-produced cheeses are also available from La Rosita (▶ 56).

LA OLIVA

The Centro de Arte Canario sells a wide range of works by local artists,

from postcards costing a few cents to originals costing up to €1,000.

LAJARES

Lajares is famous for its embroidery school, which is now part of one of the island's best *artesanías* (craft shops). You'll find it on the main road in the centre of the village. Founded in 1950, it claims to be the only original Canarian embroidery workshop on the island and is famous for its openwork embroidery tablecloths and serviettes plus lace items. The Artesanía Lajares also sells a wide range of other handicrafts, plus aloe vera products, clothing, food, wine, cheese, preserves and souvenirs.

Surfers regularly pass through Lajares en route to neighbouring El Cotillo and there are a handful of specialist surfing shops. If you need a board, suit or just a t-shirt then Witchcraft and Magma at either end of the village have some funky gear.

Where to...
Be Entertained

The beaches of Corralejo and El Cotillo are famous for their excellent water sports conditions (▶ 12–14). Corralejo is also a lively town after dark – the action is largely dispersed among its many disco and karaoke bars, sports bars and British-style pubs, although there are no "significant" nightclubs.

WATER SPORTS

For the best windsurfing and kiteboarding, go to the Playas de Corralejo (▶ 12–13) and Playa Castillo at El Cotillo.

Flag Beach Windsurf and Kitesurf Centre (tel: 928 866 389; 630 062 131, UK 0871 711 5036; www.flagbeach.com) is the north's biggest and longest-established water sports operator. It is located on Flag Beach (just look for the name in big letters on its hut, clearly visible from the main road). First-class, highly structured, friendly tuition from beginners to advanced level is available in windsurfing, surfing, bodyboarding and kitesurfing. This is the only centre where you can have a go at all these sports. Surfers will also catch a wave at El Cotillo and at the beaches west of Corralejo harbour. For diving, ▶ 27.

NIGHTLIFE

Corralejo bars and pubs play host to a lively music scene. One of the best is the Rock Island Bar at Calle Crucero Baleares (www.rockislandbar.com), with live acoustic acts every evening. Imagine is another bar dedicated to high quality live acoustic music, open nightly. Irish bands and local musicians play live nightly at Rosie O'Grady's on Calle Pizarro and at The Dubliner in the CC Atlántico.

For a full list of who's playing where see the free monthly handout, *Fuerteventura Grapevine*, available in many bars, pubs and restaurants, or visit www.fuerteventuragrapevine.net. If you're looking for a disco try the Waikiki at Avenida Hernández Morán. If tongue-in-cheek cross-dressing is your scene then Sadie's Drag Bar on Calle Isaac Peral provides a night of comedy and cabaret (Thu–Tue 8pm–2am).

EXCURSIONS

By boat

There are several boat trips, which depart from Corralejo harbour daily. A day aboard the *Catlanza* (tel: 928 513 022, www.catlanza.com), a luxury 23m (75 feet) catamaran, is highly recommended. The Anglo-Irish-Canarian crew are great fun and will take you to Lanzarote's Papagayo beaches. They offer jet ski rides and you may get to snorkel with dolphins. *Siña María* is a German-run 18m (60 feet) luxury catamaran, which specialises in seafishing and operates from Corralejo. They anchor off Lobos for snorkelling and swimming (tel: 686 725 327).

By land

If you fancy exploring the island's rocky terrain on three wheels, take out a trike with Fuertetrike (valid car driver's licence required), or be chauffeur-driven (mob: 649 938 581, www1.freewebs.com/fuertetrikes). For extra stability try a quad bike with FuerteAdventure (tel: 928 866 552, 660 099 694). No experience is needed and two people can share a bike if the combined weight is less than 115kg (18 stones). Ventura biking offer mountain bike tours ranging from 16km (10 miles) to 86km (53 miles), www.ventura-biking.com.

The Centre

Getting Your Bearings 66 – 67
In Two Days 68 – 69
Don't Miss 70 – 74
At Your Leisure 75 – 78
Where to... 79 – 84

Getting Your Bearings

The interior of Fuerteventura is home to spectacular mountain scenery and the villages of Betancuria, Vega de Río Palmas, Pájara and Antigua are the oldest and among the most picturesque on the island. You can trace their history through their beautiful churches and colonial architecture and as a bonus they also have some of the finest places to eat. While Betancuria is a monument to Fuerteventura's major historical events, the Ecomuseo de La Alcogida at Tefia is the no-less-fascinating story of how ordinary *majoreros* have eked a living from this harsh land over the last century or so. From Tefia right down to Pájara it's a joy to drive the quiet roads, stopping off at the frequent *miradores* (viewing points) to enjoy the ancient landscape.

On the east coast the proximity of the airport and the man-made resort of Caleta de Fuste means it's very popular with British holidaymakers. To the north lies the tourist-free capital of Puerto del Rosario while just south the delightful little fishing hamlet of Salinas del Carmen is worth a visit, not only for its peaceful location but also for its recently opened Salt Museum.

The west coast is wild unadulterated Fuerteventura, as exemplified by Playa de Garcey where the SS *American Star* was wrecked and the giant Caleta Negra cave north of Ajuy. Don't miss visiting these shores but never underestimate the power of the sea.

Punta del Tarajalito

Ajuy 9

Playa de la Solapa

385m
▲
Montaña Gavioto

Fayagua

FV605

Visit windmills and picturesque villages

★ Don't Miss

1. Betancuria ➤ 70
2. Antigua ➤ 73
3. Ecomuseo de La Alcogida ➤ 74

At Your Leisure

4. Los Molinos ➤ 75
5. Puerto del Rosario ➤ 75
6. Caleta de Fuste ➤ 76
7. Salinas del Carmen ➤ 76
8. Vega de Río Palmas ➤ 77
9. Ajuy ➤ 77

10. Pájara ➤ 78
11. Centro de Interpretación de los Molinos ➤ 78
12. Gran Tarajal/Las Playitas ➤ 78

The Centre of the Island in Two Days

Day One

Morning

From **6 Caleta de Fuste** head north, bypass **5 Puerto del Rosario**, drive inland towards Betancuria and Antigua on the FV20 then head north to spend the rest of the morning at the **3 Ecomuseo de La Alcogida** (➤ 74) at Tefia. Head west for a late fish lunch at **4 Los Molinos** (➤ 75).

Afternoon

Retrace your journey back to the FV20, head towards Betancuria, but after passing through Valle de Santa Inés, turn off the road towards

2 Antigua (below) and visit the **11 Centro de Interpretacíon de los Molinos** (➤ 78). The restaurant here is a showcase for authentic Canarian food but if you crave more fish and seafood hold your appetite! Head back east on the FV50 and FV2, which emerges on the coast at **7 Salinas del Carmen** (➤ 76). Visit the Salt Museum and enjoy dinner or just a drink at Los Caracolitos restaurant (➤ 81).

Day Two

Morning

Drive straight to **1 Betancuria** (above and right, ➤ 70–72) and spend the morning visiting the church (opposite page), the Museo de Arte Sacro and the Casa Santa María. Have lunch in either one of the Casa Santa María's two cafés or its restaurant or at the equally impressive Don Antonio's at **8 Vega de Río Palmas** (➤ 77).

Afternoon

Head south through Vega de Río Palmas (right) towards Pájara. Before visiting the famous church, turn right in the village centre and follow the signs to **9 Ajuy** (➤ 77) where you can walk along the shore of the very first part of the Canarian archipelago that rose from the seas millions of years ago. If you haven't eaten yet there are also good fish restaurants here. Head back to **10 Pájara** by which time the church (➤ 78) will be open and have dinner opposite here, in La Fonda restaurant (➤ 81).

General note

See also the suggested drive, which links several of the places we feature in the central part of the island (➤ 145–149).

Betancuria

Once the island capital and still retaining a real sense of history, the village of Betancuria is Fuerteventura's principal place of interest. You can see all its "sights" in a couple of hours but take your time, wander around the houses – several of which have facades and doorways dating from the 16th and 17th centuries – then linger over a coffee or a meal – Betancuria has some of the best places to eat and drink on the island – and savour the atmosphere.

The best way to approach Betancuria is from the south. Just as you enter the village, there's the famous picture-postcard view across the dry riverbed of the 17th-century church of Santa María, surrounded by a cluster of equally venerable bright white buildings streaked green by palm trees. The island conqueror, Jean de Béthencourt (▶ 9), founded his capital here in 1404, well away from the coast, with the intention of avoiding Berber pirate attacks. Unfortunately, the raiders were undeterred and in 1593 they destroyed the church and took 600 islanders as slaves. The village remained capital until 1834 but thereafter became a sleepy backwater until the advent of tourism gave it a fresh lease of life.

Iglesia de Santa María is one of the island's most beautiful churches

Iglesia de Santa María
Rebuilt in 1620, this is one of the most beautiful churches on the island, with naive-style pastel-painted side altars providing relief from the

baroque high altar. The church has Gothic arches, a wineglass-shaped pulpit, a *mudéjar* ceiling, and a Judgement Day painting. Centuries-old gravestones form part of the uneven flagged floor, and the Norman image of St Catherine is one of the oldest post-conquest relics in the archipelago. The church is no longer used for services.

The restored Casa Santa María is an island showcase

Casa Santa María

Set opposite the church, at first glance you might think that the Casa Santa María is no more than an extremely attractive restaurant and café (► 79). In fact this is just a small part of the largest house in the village, much of it dating from the 16th century and recently restored by its German owner to become an island showcase. To access the rest of the house you have to walk alongside the restaurant to the Museo Artesanía entrance. Here, beautifully arranged in a series of Spanish colonial-style wooden and stone rooms, terraces and courtyards decked with flowers and greenery, you will find island merchandise for sale, tasting areas, a video and exhibition of rural bygones, artisans at work, a cactus garden and perhaps the prettiest café on the island. Don't miss the multivision audio-visual show, which features the brilliant photography of Reiner Loos and Luis Soltmann.

Museo de Arte Sacro

This small collection of religious art is housed in the 16th-century former residence of the church authorities. Its highlights are the figure of Santiago (St James), brought by the Spanish in the hope that it might evangelise the Guanches, and the Pendón de la Conquista, Béthencourt's original flag.

The Pozo del Diablo rock in the ruins of the Convento de San Buenaventura

Convento de San Buenaventura

Set 200m (220 yards) north of the church in a gully just off the main road is the roofless ruin of the Convento de San Buenaventura. This Franciscan abbey was the oldest on the island, founded by monks who came over with the Norman conquerors. Its roof collapsed in 1836, however, and the monks moved away.

Visit the convent ruins (bottom) and sample homemade wines at the Casa Santa María (top)

Museo Arqueológico y Etnográfico

The highlight of this rather uninspiring collection of Guanche relics is its display from La Cueva de los Idolos (the Cave of the Idols) in Villaverde. Pick up a booklet from the desk, which translates the Spanish captions into other languages.

TAKING A BREAK

Go to pages 79–81 for the several restaurant options in and around Betancuria.

✚ 165 D5

Iglesia de Santa María and Museo de Arte Sacro
✉ Calle Carmelo Silvera ☎ 928 878 003 ◉ Mon–Fri 11–4:30, Sat 11–3:30 💷 Combined, inexpensive

Casa Santa María
✉ Casa Santa María Museo Artesanía (Multivision, crafts and shops)
☎ 928 878 282 ◉ Mon–Sat 11–4 💷 Expensive

Museo Arqueológico y Etnográfico
✉ Calle Roberto Roldán (main road) ☎ 928 862 342 ◉ Tue–Sat 10–5, Sun 11–2 💷 Inexpensive

BETANCURIA: INSIDE INFO

Top tip Come here **early or late** to beat the coach tours, but not on a Sunday when most things are closed.

Must see The 20-minute **Casa Santa María** Multivision audio-visual show will whet your appetite for seeing the whole island. There is no commentary (just music) so no language difficulty!

Hidden gem The bronze cannon in the front garden of the **Museo Arqueológico** was seized from the British at the Battle of Tamasite (near Tuineje). In 1740 a troop of English privateers (state-sanctioned pirates) attacked the island but were seen off by a group of 37 locals with muskets and agricultural tools. Thirty Englishmen were killed and five locals died (► 17).

2 Antigua

Antigua has many things in common with its close neighbour, Betancuria, across the mountain range. It is indeed an old (*antigua*) village, established in 1485 by settlers from Normandy and Andalucía, and it too was capital of the island, but only held that honour for a short while – either one year or 25 years, depending on which definition of capital you wish to use! Today it is a well-kept village, although it doesn't attract as many visitors as Betancuria. It does, however, have the most visited windmill on the island.

The centre of Antigua features a charming square with the pretty little white church of Nuestra Señora de Antigua, built in 1785. Hoopoes fly around the gardens in the square.

Just north of the village is the **Centro de Artesanía Molino**, a mini-village museum and exhibition centre, constructed under the supervision of Lanzarote's inspirational architect and artist César Manrique (► 108). The centrepiece is a beautifully restored 200-year-old windmill set in a cactus garden. The

Antigua boasts the most visited windmill on the island

Centro also includes a craft centre and shop, a gallery and exhibition halls devoted to ethnography and archaeology, and a pleasant little plaza with a café. Its La Molina restaurant, housed in a large reconstructed circular wood-and-stone granary, is well worth a look whether or not you intend to eat (► 79–80).

TAKING A BREAK

La Molina restaurant is perfect for a full meal or just a drink (► 79–80).

➕ 165 D5

Centro de Artesanía Molino
✉ In the village centre ☎ 928 862 342
🕐 Tue–Fri, Sun 9:30–5 💰 Inexpensive

ANTIGUA: INSIDE INFO

Top tip Some areas of the **Centro** may be closed due to staff shortages. This is also a popular venue with coach parties so it may be crowded.

One to miss The exhibition on the **Cueva de Villaverde** is only in Spanish.

3 Ecomuseo de La Alcogida

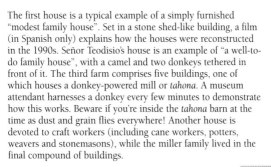

This open-air museum, set in the red-dust countryside, is a slice of rural village island life as it was some 50 to 100 years ago. There are five houses and farms to visit so allow a couple of hours to see everything.

The first house is a typical example of a simply furnished "modest family house". Set in a stone shed-like building, a film (in Spanish only) explains how the houses were reconstructed in the 1990s. Señor Teodisio's house is an example of "a well-to-do family house", with a camel and two donkeys tethered in front of it. The third farm comprises five buildings, one of which houses a donkey-powered mill or *tahona*. A museum attendant harnesses a donkey every few minutes to demonstrate how this works. Beware if you're inside the *tahona* barn at the time as dust and grain flies everywhere! Another house is devoted to craft workers (including cane workers, potters, weavers and stonemasons), while the miller family lived in the final compound of buildings.

Learn about traditional crafts and lifestyles at the Ecomuseo de La Alcogida

TAKING A BREAK

The reception area includes a dark low-ceilinged little café-bar where locals gather. You can get a drink here and perhaps a freshly baked aniseed-flavoured bread roll. The nearest recommended restaurant is at Los Molinos (➤ 80).

🕂 162 C2 ⊠ Tefía ☎ 928 878 049 🕓 Tue–Fri, Sun 9:30–5:30 💷 Moderate

ECOMUSEO DE LA ALCOGIDA: INSIDE INFO

Top tips Pick up an **audio device** with a commentary in English or German. **Take care when crossing the main road**. Not a lot of traffic comes this way but it can be fast. Also beware low roofs and do not get in the way of the *tahona* (donkey-powered mill) when it starts working!

In more detail An *alcogida* is an irrigation ditch or canal, vital in collecting and distributing what little water can be gathered by precipitation or pumped from the ground.

At Your Leisure

❹ Los Molinos

A picturesque spot, popular with locals and tourists, the little fishing village of Los Molinos is one of the few places on the island where you will see fresh running water. A footbridge crosses a shallow slow-flowing stream making its way to a small lagoon, and a flock of ducks, joined by the occasional wading bird, sits in front of the Restaurant Casa Pon. Around the corner, right on the beach, is La Terraza, another good bet for a fish lunch (➤ 80). In summer the beach is golden sand; in winter the waves wash it away to uncover black shingle. As if by magic, however, the sands return in summer.

➕ 162 C3

❺ Puerto del Rosario

Arguably the main attraction of the island capital is its nightlife (aimed at the local youth), but there are a handful of low-key sights here too. If curiosity does get the better of you, the main streets are Calle Primero Mayo and Calle León y Castillo. The town's main church is the pastel-blue Iglesia Nuestra Señora del Rosario, built in 1830. Adjacent is the **Casa Museo Unamumo**. This was formerly the modest Hotel Fuerteventura where the poet Miguel Unamuno spent most of his time on the island (➤ 76), and there is a small exhibition of memorabilia and furnishing of the period.

On the corner of Calle Primero Mayo and Calle Jesús y Mary is the Cafeteria Naufragio. Pop in here to see salvaged materials from the ill-fated luxury liner SS *American Star* (➤ 28–29).

➕ 163 E2

Casa Museo Unamuno
✉ Calle Virgen del Rosario
☎ 928 862 376
🕐 Mon–Fri 9–2 💷 Inexpensive

Boats moored in the harbour of Puerto del Rosario

The Spanish Foreign Legion

Contrary to what old guidebooks say, the Spanish Foreign Legion is no longer based in the capital. After being resident for many years they departed in 1996, largely unlamented on account of their drinking and brawling, though they still have a training barracks near the airport.

The controversial poet

Don Miguel Unamuno was born in Bilbao in 1864. In 1900 he was elected rector of Salamanca University, Spain's most distinguished seat of learning, from where he pursued his love of poetry and philosophy. Ever the outspoken republican, he was dismissed from his post because of his criticism of the king, and in March 1924 as a result of his vociferous opposition to the Spanish Premier, Primo de Rivera, he was exiled to Fuerteventura. He was here just four months before fleeing to Paris where he stayed until 1930, returning to Spain when Rivera fell from power. At the outbreak of the civil war, Unamuno sided with Franco but soon fell out with him and was placed under house arrest where he died in 1936. Despite his brief sojourn on Fuerteventura, Unamuno developed a real affinity with its Spartan beauty and simple lifestyle, "a rock thirsting in the sun....a treasure of health and honesty" and often referred to the island in his writing. As he is the only man of letters ever to be associated with Fuerteventura, the authorities have not surprisingly made a fuss of him, and his most famous quote "Fuerteventura is an oasis in the desert of civilization" has become a mantra in island guidebooks and tourist literature. A statue of Unamuno can be seen at the foot of Montaña Quemada (➤ 146).

6 Caleta de Fuste

This popular neat and tidy man-made resort mostly comprises low-rise apartments and shopping centres built around a shallow protected bay and a busy little port. It was previously known simply as El Castillo after the Castillo de Fuste, a squat black stone watchtower built in 1741, now appropriated by the Hotel Barceló as the centrepiece of an outdoor swimming pool complex. A few metres away, overlooking the port, is a black stone lighthouse.

The beach is man-made and, compared to the island's natural strands, is mediocre, but it is very family friendly and ideal for learning windsurfing. The port has a small aquarium and is the departure point for interesting sea excursions (➤ 84).

➕ 165 F5

7 Salinas del Carmen

Salinas are saltpans and have been worked at this site since the 18th century. The current pans date from 1910 and were in use until just a few years ago. They have been restored as part of the new **Museo de Sal**. Outside the museum interpretive boards tell how the salt was dried, cleaned and stored in the newly restored *almacen* (warehouse) then moved on wagons on rails into boats at the quiet little fishing hamlet just 100m (110 yards) away. Mounted above the saltpans is the eye-catching 15m-long (50 feet) skeleton of a whale, which beached here recently. The pans and the bay attract several species of wading birds.

➕ 165 F5

Museo de Sal
☎ 928 174 926 ⏰ Tue–Fri, Sun 9:30–5:30

Caleta de Fuste is a family-friendly resort

Vega de Río Palmas is one of the island's greenest spots

⑧ Vega de Río Palmas

As the name suggests, this is one of the island's most fertile valleys, dotted with mini oases of palm trees watered by scores of water pumps which delve deep beneath the baked top soil. Reservoirs are a rare sight on Fuerteventura but from a vantage point high on the main road you can spot the Embalse de la Peñitas and the little white chapel of La Virgen de la Peña (▶ 148).

The village church, the **Ermita de La Virgen de la Peña**, dates from the late 18th century and is worth a look inside. On the third Saturday in September this is the focal point for one of the island's most colourful fiestas (▶ 17).

✚ 164 C5

Ermita de la Virgen de la Peña
✉ Located in the centre of the village
🕐 Tue–Sun 11–1, 5–7

Island church interiors

The island's charming 18th-century churches (including those at Betancuria, Antigua, La Oliva and Pájara) share a number of very similar characteristics. All feature a wine glass-shaped pulpit, a painting of Christ in Majesty (with souls below in Hell), and an intricate wooden Moorish-style ceiling.

⑨ Ajuy

In 1402 the Norman invaders, led by Jean de Béthencourt, first landed on Fuerteventura. Today it is a quiet fishing village also known by the name of Puerto Peña, mostly visited for its black sand beach, popular with surfers, and its fish restaurants. The local fishing fleet only operate between May and October, as in winter the sea is too rough.

Take a walk up the steps and along the cliff edge to see how the wind and waves have carved strange patterns. Continue walking north and there are numerous caves to explore. The largest of these, the Caleta Negra, is 600m (2,000 feet) deep but unless you are experienced in caving it is dangerous to attempt to descend and even more so if the sea is rough.

✚ 164 B5

🔟 Pájara

Once voted the eighth best-kept village in all Spain, you'll find Pájara looking spick and span and a welcome burst of floral colour after the stark brown hues of the interior. It is one of the island's oldest villages, settled in the 17th century and famous for its church, Nuestra Señora de la Regla, built in 1685. The carvings on the portal depict what appear to be two native Indians in headdresses, plus stylised birds and animals. These are often referred to as Aztec-influenced and while the material and the style of carving indicate a local craftsperson, the origins of the style is a mystery.

➕ 164 C4

🔟 Centro de Interpretación de los Molinos

This area was once the "breadbasket" of the interior so it's an appropriate place for a Windmill Interpretation Centre. The exhibition is based in a lovely old restored house and garden and includes hand mills, animal-powered mills and windmills, including a full-sized one you can enter. Pick up a leaflet to translate the captions into your own language.

➕ 165 D5 ✉ Calle la Cruz 13,

Tiscamanita (Tuineje) ☎ 928 851 400
🕐 Tue–Sun 9:30–5:30 💲 Inexpensive

🔟 Gran Tarajal/Las Playitas

Although it is the second biggest town on the island after Puerto del Rosario, there is little to attract visitors to Gran Tarajal aside from a large, well-kept, black sand beach. It's better to make a beeline 6km (3.5 miles) north to the little white fishing village of Las Playitas, with less manicured dark sands but more character and popular fish restaurants.

➕ 165 D3

Off the beaten track
Pájara is the nearest village to the island's famous shipwreck SS *American Star* (➤ 28–29).

Five good fish restaurants
• Casa Victor, Las Playitas (➤ 81)
• Frasquita, Caleta de Fuste (➤ 80)
• Puerto de la Peña (Casa Pepin), Ajuy (➤ 81)
• La Terraza, Los Molinos (➤ 80)
• Los Caracolitos, Salinas del Carmen (➤ 81)

Pájara is full of colour and interesting architectural details

Where to...
Eat and Drink

Prices
Expect to pay for a three-course meal for one, excluding drinks and service

€ under €15   €€ €15–25   €€€ over €25

BETANCURIA

Casa Princess Arminda €€

Set in an atmospheric 16th-century building in the historic heart of the village, the Casa Princess Arminda features typical Canarian dishes which are mostly home made, featuring local and sometimes home-grown ingredients. Try the speciality lamb stew, packed with fresh herby flavours, and finish with the house dessert special, banana and almond cake.

➕ 165 D5 ⊠ Calle Juan de Bethencourt, 2 ☎ 928 87 89 79, www.princessarminda.com

Casa Santa María Café Bar €€

The Casa Santa María café is entered through a dark, atmospheric bar hung with impressive hams, garlic and huge cowbells. It sells home-made wines and muscatel from Lanzarote from the barrel. Two lovely sunny courtyards lead off here decorated with large pithoi, olive trees and yuccas, cacti and bright bougainvillea. The food is good and even the toilets are an architectural treat.

➕ 165 D5 ⊠ Plaza Iglesia ☎ 928 878 282 ⊙ Sep–Jun daily 11–6; Jul–Aug noon–7

Casa Santa María Café Bar (inside Museo Artesanía) €€

Take a seat on the terrace beneath a thatched parasol or under the laurel tree surrounded by bougainvillea, a lemon tree and an immaculate cactus garden. It's rather like sitting in a picture postcard complete with smiling waitress in traditional dress. Snacks include smoked pork fillet, Lanzarote smoked salmon and mackerel fillets.

➕ 165 D5 ⊠ Plaza Iglesia ☎ 928 878 282 ⊙ Mon–Sat 11–4. [Note: you have to pay to get into the Museo Artesanía (▶ 73) but it is well worth the admission.]

Casa Santa María Restaurant €€€

The Casa Santa María Restaurant is in the dining room of a gloriously restored 16th-century farmhouse. Antiques abound though don't overpower and the food is first class, although it can be expensive (there is a daily set menu at a more reasonable price). Start with dates in bacon or fresh cheese baked with tomatoes and garlic. House specials are lamb and kid and a range of local dishes. Finish with a banana flambé or a tooth-melting *crema canaria* with *bienmesabe*.

➕ 165 D5 ⊠ Plaza Iglesia ☎ 928 878 282 ⊙ Sep–Jun daily 11–6; Jul–Aug noon–7

Val Tarajal €€

This traditional dark-wood restaurant has few frills except for a giant 4m (13 foot) long *timple* (Canarian five-string ukulele-like instrument) on one wall! All the usual Canarian favourites are on the menu but if you want *puchero* or *sancocho* (▶ 21) you'll have to come on Sunday or public holidays.

➕ 165 D5 ⊠ Calle Roberto Roldán 6 (main road) ☎ 928 878 007 ⊙ Tue–Sun 11–5

ANTIGUA

La Molina €€

It feels almost as if you are stepping inside a huge windmill as you enter this large round building. In fact, it used to be a granary. It has been beautifully restored with brown and white giraffe-patterned bare stone walls and gleaming woodwork. Rustic candelabras have been made from inverted clay pots riddled with holes through which the light shines, and with Canarian music playing in the background this completes the ambience. The food is upmarket traditional island cuisine. Start with fried cheese with *mojo verde* or *carpaccio* of tuna. Then try goat stew or *cazuela de pescadores*, a special fish stew. Tourist groups often come here.

☐ 165 D5 ☒ Carretera de Antigua km20 ☎ 928 878 577 ☉ Tue–Fri, Sun 10–6, meals noon–3

PUERTO DEL ROSARIO

Hotel Fuerteventura Playa Blanca €€€

The Hotel Fuerteventura was until recently a *parador* (state-run hotel) and therefore responsible for serving the very best in regional food. Even

now, it's still an interesting old place to sample traditional Canarian food in a quiet formal atmosphere overlooking the beach of Playa Blanca and with views across the bay to Puerto del Rosario.

☐ 163 E2 ☒ Calle Playa Blanca 42 ☎ 928 851 150 ☉ Daily 7:30–10:30, 3:30–10:30

LA ASOMADA

(near Puerto del Rosario)

La Casa del Jamón €€–€€€

This splendid family-run shop-cum-restaurant is a treat for Spanish food and wine buffs and, of course, lovers of Spain's many famous *jamones* (hams). Its rustic Spanish country-style restaurant serves typical Canarian meals plus dishes from the Basque and Navarra regions that you probably won't find anywhere else on the island. The desserts are delicious and the wine list is extensive.

☐ 163 D2 ☒ La Asomada (sign-posted just off the main Tetir-La Oliva

road and off the Carretera del Sur, 5km (3 miles) west of Puerto del Rosario) ☎ 928 530 064 ☉ Daily 1–5

LOS MOLINOS

La Terraza €€

This is the best of the two fish restaurants in this pretty little fishing village and, unlike its neighbour, it enjoys a grandstand view over the beach. There's not much sophistication here, with plastic tables and chairs, but the service is good.

☐ 162 C3 ☒ Los Molinos ☉ Wed–Mon noon–7

CALETA DE FUSTE

Frasquita €€

"Only Fresh Fish" is the motto at this rustic no-frills whitewashed landmark beachside restaurant on the opposite side of the bay from the port. Choose your fish from a tray brought to you by the waiter – it's unlikely to be

expensive and the best quality is guaranteed.

☐ 165 F5 ☒ Playa Caleta de Fuste ☎ 928 163 657 ☉ Tue–Sun 1–4, 6–10

Gambrinus €€

Nominally a *cervecería* ("beer house") with an old beer lorry outside and with a beery feel to its dark wood-panelled interior, Gambrinus is actually a large smart modern restaurant with rather formal pink tablecloths and wicker furniture that spill out onto a terrace. Steaks on hot stones and flambés are the specialities but you'll be equally welcome for tapas, pizza, a cocktail or just a beer. Live music daily in summer.

☐ 165 F5 ☒ CC Broncemar ☎ 928 163 555 ☉ Daily 9am–11pm

La Molina Bar Terraza €€

This friendly little conservatory-style diner, set just back from the beach, is run by locals who offer home-made Canarian dishes and tapas (not easy to find in Caleta), as well as international and Spanish food. A veranda at the back opens onto a pleasant children's play area.

➕ 165 F5 ⊠ Calle Pitera (by CC El Castillo car park) 🕐 Thu–Tue 9am–11pm, Sat–Sun 9am–11:30pm

Restaurante Puerto Castillo €€€

The restaurant entrance is at the foot of the lighthouse and although there is no access to the very top, book a table on the front row of the large first-floor balcony which looks out over the port and you have the best seat in Caleta. This is a smart place with formal but friendly service, specialising in steaks and traditional meaty Canarian dishes such as shoulder of lamb and goat stew.

➕ 165 F5 ⊠ Muelle del Castillo ☎ 928 163 877 🕐 Mon–Sat 12:30–11

SALINAS DEL CARMEN

Los Caracolitos €€

This attractive little modern restaurant sits almost right on the beach of this tiny fishing hamlet. There is a reasonable choice of fish and seafood dishes on the menu but if you want to go local start with the home-made fish croquettes then ask for the catch of the day. The staff are friendly and helpful.

➕ 165 F5 ⊠ Salinas del Carmen ☎ 928 174 242 🕐 Mon–Sat noon–11 🗓 No credit cards

VEGA DE RÍO PALMAS

Don Antonio €€€

Housed in a lilac-trimmed colonial house opposite the church, this German-owned restaurant is not only pretty from without, but also from within – its courtyard and dining rooms are stunning. It may be the most expensive (non-hotel) restaurant on the island but the food and surroundings are unbeatable. A short menu of nouvelle international-Canarian-Spanish dishes changes daily. Gourmets with deep wallets will appreciate the *menu*

degustación (selection of dishes) of five or seven courses.

➕ 164 C5 ⊠ Plaza Iglesia ☎ 928 878 757 🕐 Tue–Sun 10–5

AJUY

Puerto de la Peña (Casa Pepín) €€

Either of the two restaurants on the front at Ajuy are fine for fresh fish and seafood but, if you would like to eat with the locals, try the Puerto de la Peña. It has the added ingredient of Pepín, a colourful local character who will (normally) be delighted to show you the interior of his house.

➕ 164 B5 ⊠ Puerto Aziel ☎ 928 161 529, 628 671 004 🕐 Daily 10–5

PÁJARA

Bar Restaurant La Fonda €€

Just across the road from the church, La Fonda is patronised by locals who drink in its rustic bar and tourists who eat outside beneath the trees.

There's a selection of tapas and Canarian favourites to choose from including house specials *carne mechada* (slices of sirloin), *conejo en adobo* (marinated rabbit) and *garbanzos compuestos* (chickpea stew).

➕ 164 C4 ⊠ Calle Nuestra Señora de Regla ☎ 928 161 625 🕐 Mon–Fri 9–6, Sat–Sun 9–9

LAS PLAYITAS

Casa Victor €€

This is by no means the most attractive restaurant in Las Playitas but even when the rest of the village is deserted Victor's is buzzing. It's set back from the front and has indoor dining only so it has to try that bit harder in terms of quality of food – fish and seafood being the staple items. A widespread reputation and a mixed clientele of locals, businessmen and tourists seem to indicate they have got it right.

➕ 165 D3 ⊠ Calle Juan Soler 22 ☎ 928 870 910 🕐 Tue–Sun noon–5, 8–11

Where to...
Stay

Prices

Expect to pay per double room, per night

€ under €60   €€ €60–90   €€€ €91–120   €€€€ over €120

Note that many of the larger hotels and apartments in Caleta de Fuste are block booked by big tour operators.

ANTIGUA

Hotel Era de la Corte €€–€€€

This beautiful *hotel rural* dates from 1890 and has been lovingly restored by the owner, Andrés (who was born here), and his wife, Victoria, who runs the kitchen, rustling up delicious Canarian specialities. All 12 rooms are individually furnished and have their own style and personality; several have four-poster beds.

The ever-helpful Andrés is extremely knowledgeable on island life and has a small library specialising in Canary Island history, flora and fauna, where guests can relax with a book and a glass of wine.

There are two small swimming pools, a solarium, garden and floodlit tennis court. Bicycles are available for rent; games provided include petanque, darts and table tennis. Breakfast is included in the price of the room.

➕ 165 D5 ✉ Calle La Corte 1 ☎ 928 878 705, 928 878 708, 📠 928 878 705, 928 878 708, www.eradelacorte.com

CALETA DE FUSTE

Hotel Elba Palace Golf €€€€

The island's first 5-star hotel, located within the Golf Club Fuerteventura (▶84), features every mod con but is designed in classic Canarian style. Its large inner courtyard is decked with palms and wooden balconies and even the staff uniform is based on traditional 18th-century Canarian dress. Its 51 bedrooms are luxurious, designed with local touches, and guest facilities include two large swimming pools, a floodlit tennis (or paddle tennis) court, jacuzzi, sauna, steam bath and beauty treatments plus a gourmet restaurant.

➕ 165 F5 ✉ Urb. Fuerteventura Golf Club ☎ 928 163 922, www.hoteleselba.com

Barceló Club El Castillo €€€€

Get the best of both worlds by staying in pretty little white apartments in lush manicured gardens right on the sea front, with the back-up of a huge resort-hotel. This comes complete with an extensive entertainment programme, bars, restaurants, pizzeria, creperie, ice cream shop, jacuzzi, thalassotherapy; a choice of five pools including the pretty one by the 18th-century Castillo (▶76) and a wide range of sports facilities including mini-golf, tennis, paddle tennis and 5-a-side football courts.

➕ 165 F5 ✉ Caleta de Fuste s/n ☎ UK 0845 090 3071; rest of Europe 0034 902 101 001, www.barceloclubelcastillo.com

PÁJARA

Hotel Rural Casa Isaítas €€

This charming, friendly, small hotel, set just outside the village, has four rooms simply furnished in "minimalist-rustic" style. Facilities include a library, internet access and a living room. Its restaurant is open to non-residents and is recommended. Breakfast is included.

➕ 164 C4 ✉ Calle Guize 7 ☎ 928 161 402, www.casaisaitas.com

Where to...
Shop

BETANCURIA

Despite its name, the Museo Artesanía in the Casa Santa María is one of the best one-stop souvenir and gift shops on the island. It features tasting areas and beautiful displays of food and drink. They sell all kinds of Canarian handicrafts. For ceramics, look in the Ceramica Casa Santa María, a busy little shop that is part of the same enterprise but has a different entrance (on the side street leading to the Museo Sacro).

Another good place for handicrafts is the Centro Insular de Artesanía on the main road.

On the southern edge of the village is the Casa de Queso (House of Cheese), a mini-supermarket selling a range of cured meats and cheeses. There is another branch

nearby at Valle de Sant Inés with a pleasant café attached.

Island handicraft centres

There are a number of Centros Insular de Artesanía (government-funded Island Handicraft Centres) around the island, the largest one being at the Centro Molino at Antigua. These are often set in an historic building and feature a range of typical island crafts. Items are often expensive but remember they are handmade, often requiring several hours' labour.

ANTIGUA

The craft shop here is one of the best on the island. New Age music lulls you while browsing the beautiful (but very expensive) leather bags, craft jewellery, super-sized wooden geckoes, silkscreen and parchment pictures and some lovely pottery pieces.

Food and drink from Spain

The Casa del Jamon (House of Ham) is in a class of its own if you are

looking for wines and comestibles. They stock around 10,000 bottles of wine (from the mainland and from all over the Canaries), liqueurs and *aguardientes* (brandies) as well as a huge range of tinned and preserved foods. They also specialise in *majorero* cheese and, of course, ham! If you can't wait to get home to taste the goods there's a restaurant on site.

PUERTO DEL ROSARIO

Puerto del Rosario caters solely for islanders. If you want to see what the locals are buying take a stroll along Calle Primero de Mayo and Calle Leon y Castillo, though most of the shops are old-fashioned and uninspiring. On the second Sunday of each month (10:30–2:30) a craft market, "Vega de Tetir", is held in the village of Tetir 8km (5 miles) west of Puerto del Rosario, selling leather goods, textiles, pottery, food and other local items. Folklore activities are also staged and may include music, dancing and camel rides.

CALETA DE FUSTE

Despite, or perhaps because of its many shopping centres, the standard of shopping in this popular resort is mediocre and usually price driven. Riu Parfum in the CC Castillo Plaza is the best bet for perfumes.

The island market (▶42) comes to Caleta on Saturday morning.

Fuerteventura is famous for its goat's cheese and has even succeeded in registering a Denominación de Origen classification (similar to the French Appellation Contrôlée wine system) to protect it from imitations. You can usually buy it in one of three ways: *natural*, its rind rubbed with oil to preserve it; *pimenta*, its rind rubbed with red *pimenta* (chilli pepper); or *gofio*, coated in toasted cornmeal.

Where to...
Be Entertained

Nightlife

The only real disco/nightclub in Caleta de Fuste is Whiskis in the Castillo Centro. Just outside the centre is a multiplex cinema and a tenpin bowling alley.

Puerto del Rosario has the best nightclubs on the island. Try Templo (Calle Teniente Durán), or Camelot (Calle León y Castillo 12). There are 90 different beers to choose from at the Heineken Bar (Calle León y Castillo 146). La Tierra (Calle Eustaqio Gopar) has live jazz on Friday and Saturday.

CALETA DE FUSTE

Golf

The Golf Club Fuerteventura, the island's original course, is just south of Caleta de Fuste (Carretera de Jandia, km11; tel: 928 160 034, www.fuerteventuragolfclub.com). It features two rounds of nine holes and several fiendish water hazards. It is host to the Spanish Canarian Open championship. Practice facilities include a 50-bay driving range and a large putting green. No handicap is required. There are plenty of facilities for non golfers who can enjoy a sauna, work out at the gym, take a leisurely swim in the swimming pool, or have a game of paddle tennis.

The island's second 18-hole golf course is the Golf Club Salinas de Antigua (tel: 928 879 444, www.salinasgolf.com), which opened in 2006. It can be found on the main road heading south, Carretera Jandia, km12. On site are a golf school and a restaurant.

Sea excursions

The most interesting of these is the Oceanarium Explorer based in Caleta de Fuste. Before setting sail you visit an aquarium where there are sharks and rays and an octopus that has been taught to unscrew a glass jar. After exploring the aquarium, you can then either set sail on a catamaran, which claims regular sightings of marine life, or take a glass bottom "submarine" (which actually stays on the surface). As a bonus you are accompanied by Harley, one of only a very few sea lions in the world trained to take commands in open waters.

Water sports

The sheltered bay of Caleta de Fuste is an ideal place to take your first windsurfing lessons. The Fanatic Fun Centre will get you going.

For diving contact the German-led Deep Blue, who have 20 years experience here (tel: 928 163 712, www.deep-blue-diving.com).

Go-karting

The Tamaretilla Karting Club offers a 1,500m (1,635 yards) adult circuit and shorter courses for juniors and children. It is near the village of Cardón, close to Tuineje (tel: 620 504 399).

Horseriding

The Finca Crines del Viento stables at Triquivijate, near Antigua, offers rides suitable for beginners and experienced riders. The staff speak English and German (tel: 609 001 141).

Bike tours

Quad bikes and trail bikes are available for hire from the English-run Backtrax (tel: 928 160 206). For details of their off-road motorbike tours suitable for beginners through to riders with years of experience, visit www.isango.com and key in your destination and select which off-road activities you are interested in. Quad bike tours also run from the Barceló hotel, in Caleta de Fuste.

The South

Getting Your Bearings 86 – 87
In Three Days 88 – 89
Don't Miss 90 – 95
At Your Leisure 96 – 99
Where to... 100 – 106

Getting Your Bearings

La Pared (literally, "the wall"), the start of the isthmus, is both the historical boundary – where the ancient wall that divided the island's two kingdoms once stood (▶10) – and an important "geo-tourism" frontier. North of here the sands are volcanic black, a daunting prospect to most holidaymakers, but almost immediately south, beginning at Costa Calma, the longest, most famous and most beautiful golden-blonde beaches in the Canaries stretch for over 30km (18 miles).

The new face of the south is Costa Calma, a man-made resort bristling with large modern hotels and shopping centres. Further west, Jandía Playa is a similar development. Yet neither of these is typical of the peninsula, which remains the island's wildest and least developed region. The north (Barlovento) coast has not a single development nor even village worthy of the name. This is a truly wild place, difficult to access but well worth the effort.

Today the road to Morro Jable is the focus of construction works. Fast straight roads and 30m-high (100 feet) bridges will make short work of the deep gullies which slow traffic to a zigzag crawl. The distance from north to south, in driving time at least, is shortening. For most holidaymakers, Morro Jable, an attractive spot with local life and a gorgeous beach, is the end of the line, and despite the new road-building programme will remain so for many years.

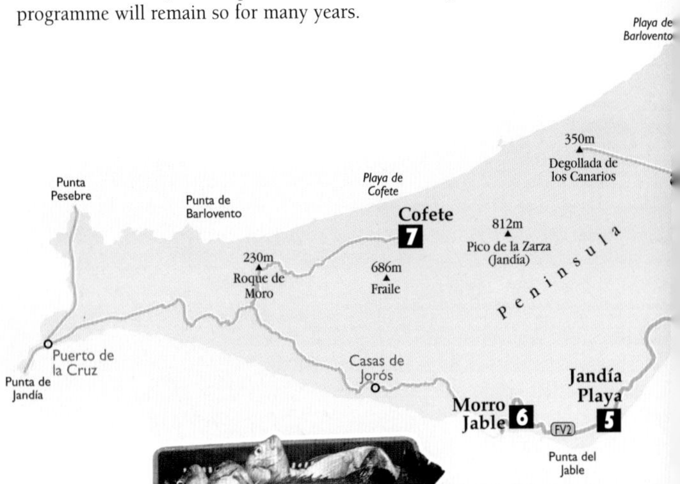

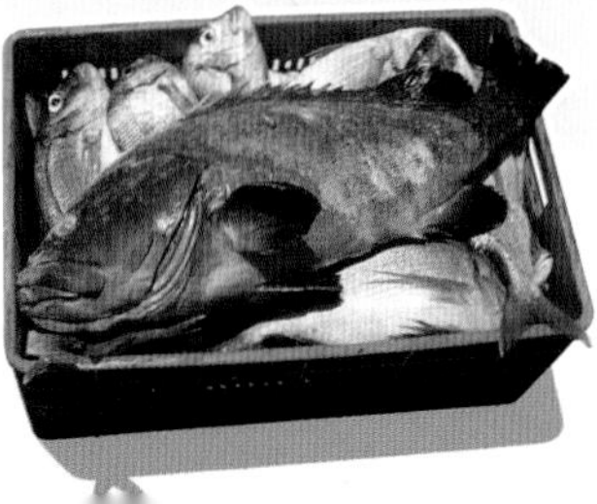

Playa de Barlovento

350m
Degollada de los Canarios

Punta Pesebre

Punta de Barlovento

Playa de Cofete

Cofete **7**

812m
Pico de la Zarza (Jandía)

230m
Roque de Moro

686m
Fraile

p e n i n s u l a

Puerto de la Cruz

Punta de Jandía

Casas de Jorós

Jandía Playa **5**

Morro Jable **6** FV2

Punta del Jable

★ Don't Miss

1 Playas de Jandía
(Jandía beaches)
➤ 90

2 La Lajita Oasis Park
➤ 93

At Your Leisure

3 La Pared ➤ 96
4 Costa Calma ➤ 96
5 Jandía Playa ➤ 96
6 Morro Jable ➤ 97
7 Cofete ➤ 98

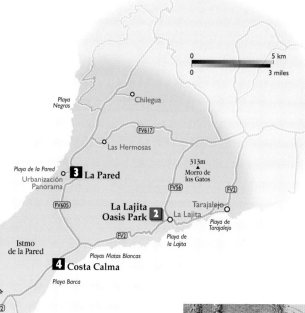

Popular places to visit
include Morro Jable's
beaches and (right)
La Lajita Oasis Park

The South
in Three Days

Note: because there is only one major road (the FV2) that links most places of interest in the peninsula, it is difficult to set out touring itineraries that do not involve backtracking. If you intend to explore north or west of Morro Jable then you will need a 4WD or Jeep-type off-road vehicle.

Day One
Morning

Set out early, steal a march on the tour buses and arrive at **2 La Lajita Oasis Park** (► 93–95) just as it opens at 9am. See all the shows and take lunch at the park in the Botanical Gardens area.

Afternoon

Drive north on the FV56 for 3–4km (2–3 miles)and turn left towards La Pared passing through the hamlet of Las Hermosas. As the road approaches the coast there are tremendous views of the wild Barlovento coastline. At **3 La Pared** (► 96) you can play a nine-hole round of golf or sunbathe at the nearby Playa de la Pared (though swimming here is dangerous) and then enjoy an evening meal at El Camello (► 100).

Day Two
Morning

Make your way to the El Palmeral centre on the main road at **4 Costa Calma** (► 96) (below, and opposite top) and either walk or drive (you'll need

an off-road vehicle) across the isthmus to the north coast following the route on pages 150–152. Return, have lunch at the Fuerte Action bar (➤ 101) and browse in the shops here.

Afternoon

Head south for 3–4km (2–3 miles) and turn left to Risco del Paso where you can spend the rest of the day on the most famous stretch of ❶ **beach** (➤ 90–91) (above) in the archipelago. You can windsurf with the experts or simply soak up the rays but remember to take your own shade along with you.

Day Three

Morning

You'll need an off-road vehicle and a sense of adventure for this excursion! Drive south past Morro Jable and take the signs to Cofete. After around 20km (12 miles) you will arrive at a pass where stupendous views of the Barlovento coast make all the effort worthwhile. Continue for another 4km (2.5 miles) into this remarkable landscape and you reach journey's end, the ramshackle hamlet of ❼ **Cofete** (➤ 98–99) where you can get a rustic but enjoyable fish lunch.

Afternoon

Make your way back to "civilisation" at ❻ **Morro Jable** (➤ 97–98). Follow the signs to the Centro Urbano, park near the square in the old part of the village and spend the rest of the afternoon on the golden beach. Have dinner in one of the many restaurants or cafés on the square (➤ 102).

Playas de Jandía

The beaches of Jandía are arguably Fuerteventura's greatest natural asset and certainly its most potent marketing tool. Water sports lovers, beach bums, families and naturists are all drawn here. Even if you have never been to Fuerteventura you've probably seen that picture, that glorious dreamy blue lagoon beach that could be the Caribbean, the Seychelles or any of the world's most exotic places. Its broody mountain backdrop with not a single hotel nor even a beach hut in sight is picture-postcard perfect. More rolls of film have been spent on the Sotavento than on any other beach in the Canary Islands and, even if most people haven't quite placed it yet, this is without doubt one of the most beautiful strands in Europe. And it is just part of a stunning coastline that stretches all the way around the Jandía peninsula.

The Sotavento coast

The Playas de Jandía begins, with a whisper, in Costa Calma. Beyond the rows of blue-and-orange beach umbrellas and loungers the beach starts to broaden out, and at Playa Barca, by the landmark Meliá

Gorriones hotel, it becomes
extraordinary. Giant dunes rear out of
black volcanic outcrops. A sandbar
stretches for 5km (3 miles) to Risco
del Paso, taming the waves, making
it perfect for families and novice
windsurfers. The shallow waters are
a dozen ever-changing shades of blue
and turquoise, gently lapping the golden-
blonde streaks of sand. At Risco del Paso there is
a beach bar, a water sports centre and a scattering of
pretty white bungalows set well back from the beach on the
low cliffs that form a backdrop. Walk along the beach for a
couple of hundred metres and you will come to another
favourite picture-postcard subject as a huge white dune and
black volcanic cliffs tumble down to the sea. It is much easier
to see where the Sotavento beach ends when you are high
above, on the main road, as it is effectively marked by an
unofficial *mirador*. From here you can enjoy the classic view.

**The Playas de
Jandía are
picture-
postcard
perfect and
great for kite-
karting**

Barlovento and Sotavento
All the beaches on the 30km-long (18 mile) southeast-
facing coast from Costa Calma to Morro Jable are
Sotavento, meaning leeward, though in fact the term
Playa de Sotavento is only applied to a single small
stretch. Similarly, the corresponding northwest-facing
beaches of the peninsula are Barlovento or windward
side, even though the term is only given to one stretch.
    Never swim on the Barlovento coastline, as even if the
waters look calm there are treacherous undercurrents.

The next 3–4km (2–3 miles) of sands is known as the Playa de Butihondo, still backed by low cliffs and shared by a number of large hotels and the German-owned holiday club resorts of Robinson and Aldiana. Set in manicured grounds they keep a discrete distance and so preserve the integrity of the beach. As the coastline turns "the corner" from facing southeast to due south it takes on its third name, Playa del Matorral. The *matorral* (vegetation) in question is crossed by a number of boardwalks. The cliffs have disappeared by the time you get to Jandía Playa. Its landmark lighthouse (► 96–97) is impressive and, once past the resort, there is a final glorious flourish as once again the cliffs and dunes return and a beautiful promenade offers great views of the broad golden beach. This tapers down to end by the little square in Morro Jable and, for most people, this is the end of the Jandía beaches.

Morro Jable's beaches are some of the most popular

Beyond the Sotavento

From here onwards you need a 4WD vehicle to explore the rest of the peninsula. By far the most popular drive, albeit a real bone-cruncher of a journey, is north to Cofete (► 98) where there is a fabulous long, untouched, empty golden beach. Northeast of here is the equally impressive Playa de Barlovento. Few people make it this far and nudity is the norm.

The easy way to visit the beaches of the northern coastline is to cross the peninsula at its narrowest point at Costa Calma, either by walking or by 4WD vehicle, following the simple route mapped out on pages 150–152.

TAKING A BREAK

There are good beach huts on two of the most attractive parts of the 30km-long (18 mile) Sotavento beach, at Morro Jable (a five- to ten-minute walk from the centre) and at Risco del Paso.

➕ 164 A2

PLAYAS DE JANDÍA: INSIDE INFO

Top tip Only at Costa Calma and part of Morro Jable will you find **beach shades** for rental. Anywhere else you will soon fry without some protection so invest in a parasol and, if you have small children, consider a small beach tent.

Getting there There are no signs to "Sotavento Beach". However, the start of it, the Playa Barca (Meliá Gorriones Hotel), is marked, as is the end, Risco del Paso. It's best to park at **Risco del Paso**. Keep your eyes peeled and your speed down as neither turn-off is particularly prominent.

2 La Lajita Oasis Park

Oasis Park is the island's biggest, best and longest-running tourist attraction. It was established in 1985 as a small garden centre and even today first impressions are less a zoo than an oasis of vivid greenery and vibrant-coloured plants set in the middle of a barren red desert.

The Animal Park
The most interesting thing about this area is not so much its inhabitants, but the setting of their enclosures along narrow shady tracks with dense foliage, brightly coloured plants (more than 6,800 varieties!) and running water. Children in particular will feel like jungle explorers. Among the hundreds of reptiles, primates and mammals and over 200 species of birds are crocodiles, tamarind monkeys, chimpanzees, meerkats, capybaras, toucans, turacos, ostriches, flamingos and pelicans.

The park is an oasis in the middle of a barren red desert

Animal and bird shows
The parrot and sea lion shows are great fun for children even if some adults may take exception to what they see as unnatural behaviour. Whatever, you won't doubt the courage of the crocodile tamer as he puts his head within inches of bone-crushing jaws. The birds of prey

show draws on the park's large collection of raptors, which for one reason or another can sadly no longer survive in the wild, and has rather more educational over entertainment content. The sea lion show is great fun and there are also reptile-handling demonstrations.

Camel breeding

Camels were introduced to the islands in 1405 by the Normans (► 25) but by 1985 they had dwindled almost to extinction, numbering less than three dozen in total. Oasis Park is hoping to reintroduce herds of the true *camello majorero* (Fuerteventuran camel) by breeding the very few that are left with African dromedaries. The park also plans to set up the first camel milk dairy in Europe. High in protein, mineral and vitamin C content, but low in cholesterol, camel milk is said to be good for the liver and the complexion.

The herd here is now 220-strong and a visit to see the beautiful baby camels is highly recommended.

Camel rides

For most visitors this is a highlight of a visit to the park and involves two people being slung, one either side of the camel, in a yoke-like wooden seat reminiscent of a funfair ride. The ride is smooth and pleasant and ascends a steep hill with excellent views of the park gardens and out to sea. There is an extra charge for rides.

Botanic Garden

Set on a steep hillside in artfully arranged gardens of black volcanic pumice particles, this collection of over 2,300 different types of cactus, succulents and indigenous plants is one of the largest and most interesting in Europe. Don't be deterred if the prospect of a cactus garden seems literally and figuratively a dry idea. From dainty little ground-hugging plants with bright yellow and shocking pink flowers and soft downy spines to classic Mexican giants with

You can watch the crocodiles being fed...

needles that could skewer someone's hand, there's every kind of cactus under the sun here.

Out of Africa
A massive new African Savannah area has giraffes, antelopes and endangered African animals including rhinoceroses, though no big cats or other predators.

TAKING A BREAK
The park has three excellent restaurants.

➕ 164 B3 ✉ Carretera General de Jandía (FV2 km 57.4), La Lajita ☎ 902 400 434, www.lajitaoasispark.com ⏰ Daily 9–6 💶 Expensive. Separate charge for camel rides. Combined ticket available

...and see ostriches, tropical birds and plenty of camels

LA LAJITA OASIS PARK: INSIDE INFO

Top tips The **camel breeding** area is off the main track and may be closed to the general public. Call in advance and you may be allowed special access. Arrive first thing in the cool of the early morning before the coach operators arrive and **wear comfortable shoes** – it's a long walk to see everything.

Hidden gem Keep your eyes peeled in the free-flying bird aviary for a **large chameleon**.

In more detail The yoke-like camel seat that accommodates two people is called *la silla inglesa*, the English chair, as it was specially designed for saddle-sore English tourists in the 19th century. An original handmade wooden *silla inglesa* is now a prized antique fetching well over €2,000 at auction!

Getting in If you are travelling independently you will park by the main zoo entrance. The **Jardín Botánico** is some 700m (770 yards) away, which can be a long hot tiring walk so return to your car and drive there.

Must see The **giraffes**, the **Botanic Garden**, the **baby camels** and the **crocodile show**.

At Your Leisure

🔞 La Pared

The site of the wall that once divided the island into two ancient kingdoms (► 10), La Pared today is home to an upmarket, largely German-populated *urbanización* (residential development). From the road above the village you can pick out the bizarre sight of bright green target circles on a black lava background. These are the greens of a nine-hole practice golf course (► 106). La Pared is also home to El Camello, one of the island's most attractive restaurants (► 100). Drive a little further north on the FV605 past the village turn-off and a superb panorama of the north coast opens out before you.

➕ 164 B3

🔞 Costa Calma

Built from scratch as an upmarket resort in the late 1970s and 1980s, Costa Calma is a disparate collection of shopping centres and large resort hotels that share the same golden sandy beach. This is the start of the famous Playa de Sotavento (► 90–91), though it is by no means the nicest stretch, where building continues apace.

➕ 164 B2

🔞 Jandía Playa

The ugly duckling of the south, this man-made mostly German-speaking resort is a cluster of large hotels and shopping centres facing onto the least interesting stretch of the Playa Matorral. The towering Faro (lighthouse) de Morro Jable was built at the turn of the 20th century and is the largest on the island. The only other point of interest here is the small zoo in the gardens of the Hotel Stella Canaris (open daily 10–6,

Unusual architecture

Although much of the new architecture of the south (particularly its hotels) is instantly forgettable or completely out of place, there are three striking examples of truly individual properties that merit more than a second glance.

First, just north of Esquinzo stands a fantasy "gingerbread" house straight from the Brothers Grimm tales that sits almost next door to the ungainly Club Paraíso Playa Sunrise Beach Hotel.

Second, looking down on Costa Calma at its northern extremity is what appears to be a large church on top of a hill. In fact, it is part of the beautifully crafted Old-Spain pueblo (village)-style hotel of Rio Calma (pictured above).

Third, at the southern end of Costa Calma is the extraordinary "space pod" complex of the Risco del Gato hotel (► 103), which was actually one of the pioneer accommodations in the south.

inexpensive). A beautifully landscaped new promenade stretches from Jandía Playa to Morro Jable (➤ below).

🚩 164 A1

6 Morro Jable

This popular resort is the end of the line of Sotavento beaches (➤ 90–91) and features one of its best stretches. The broad golden sands, known as the Playa de Cebada (Barley Beach), are backed by a large dune and low cliffs, have lots of space and excellent facilities for sun worshippers including parasols and loungers for hire, a good beach bar and gleaming new stainless steel-and-glass toilet and shower facilities. Fluorescent coloured windsurfers complete a picture-postcard scene. There's a great view of it all from the beautiful new promenade, lined with bright bougainvillea and antique-style street furniture. This runs from the original town centre to the neighbouring resort of Jandía Playa. Look up to the cliff and you can see the big hotels where most people stay here.

The old centre of Morro Jable is reached by any of a number of narrow streets, which dive down to the sea across a dry riverbed. Right on the seafront a dozen or so bars and restaurants cluster in an attractive lively jumble around a couple of small squares. At the heart

For kids
- La Lajita Oasis Park (➤ 93–95), particularly the animal shows
- The Subcat submarine (➤ 106)
- A water banana ride at Jandía Playa (➤ 106)
- Learning to windsurf with René Egli (➤ 106)

Relax on the broad golden sands (above) and see the island's largest lighthouse, both at Morro Jable (top)

Off-road driving

While it is a fact that thousands of tourists do travel on the dirt tracks beyond Morro Jable in ordinary hire cars, it is not recommended to attempt this kind of off-road driving in anything other than a 4WD or Jeep-style vehicle. If it has recently rained heavily, don't even consider driving beyond Morro Jable in an ordinary car.

Three best Canarian meals

- El Camello, La Pared (➤ 100)
- Marabú, Esquinzo (➤ 101)
- Posada San Borondon, Costa Calma (➤ 101)

of the main square is *El Viejo Vapor* (The Old Steamer), a real section of a steamship complete with funnel which used to house a restaurant but is, for the time being at least, vacant.

The port of Morro Jable, just south of the centre, is home to the local fishing fleet, scheduled ferry and jetfoil sailings to Gran Canaria and Tenerife, plus leisure excursions.

🔲 **165 F1**

🔳 Cofete

The road to Cofete begins promisingly, just south of Morro Jable, with brand new asphalt roads.

Alas, these last barely 3km (2 miles) and then it is another 24km (15 miles) of teeth-rattling spine-jolting dirt-track driving. The last part of the journey, on little more than single-track hairpin bends with unprotected drops, is truly hair-raising! Slow down, use your horn on blind bends and be very careful. As you pass the highest point of the journey between the mountains of Pico de la Zarza (the island's highest peak) at 812m (2,663 feet), and Pico de la Fraile at 686m (2,250 feet), your reward is a view far along the northwest coast that will linger long in your memory. This is an awesome landscape unchanged in eons, on which man has made very little impression. The ramshackle hamlet of Cofete with its café-restaurant is for many people the end of the line. Here they enjoy a well-earned cup of coffee, perhaps a meal and head back with a satisfying "been there, seen it" feeling. More intrepid explorers venture down to the magnificent but dangerous beaches and even further afield. From the restaurant you can look out to the mansion of Gustav Winter (see opposite), which sits isolated and brooding beneath the mountains. Low clouds often hang menacingly here and there is a real sense of drama. Little wonder that this has become the most talked about house on the island. Although it is

The sandy shore of Playa Barca on the Sotovento coast

The mystery of the Winter mansion

Gustav Winter was born in Germany in 1893. He spent many years as an engineer in Spain and settled in Jandía in the early 1930s. It is well documented that in 1938 he met Admiral Wilhem Canaris, head of German military intelligence, to discuss a project, which subsequently involved German workers coming to Jandía. In 1940 construction began on the Villa Winter and in 1941 the authorities in Madrid officially assigned the whole peninsula of Jandía to the administration of Gustav Winter. Shortly after this it became a closed military zone. What subsequently happened at the Villa Winter is unknown but certainly during the war U-boats were frequent visitors to Fuerteventura, refuelling here despite Spain's supposed neutrality, and divers on the island today tell of a U-boat wreck lying in 200m (650 feet) of water very close to Cofete.

Gustav Winter died in 1971 and never revealed the mysteries of the mansion. However, it is also well documented that Franco and Hitler were unofficial allies and Admiral Canaris had been involved in building secret submarine bases before his meeting with Winter. So, it is hard not to speculate that this was the primary purpose. It is said that tunnels lead from the house to the beach and that submarines were also used to transport fleeing Nazis to South America at the end of the war. There is no evidence to support this claim but as the house has never been explored by outside parties it may still have tales to tell.

There is no formal admission to the house but talk to the locals in Cofete and someone will be pleased to show you inside.

only a short drive to the mansion do not attempt it unless you have a 4WD vehicle as the road is very bumpy indeed.

➕ 165 E2

Tourist offices
Jandía Playa
➕ 164 A1 ✉ CC Cosmo
☎ 928 540 776
🕐 Mon–Fri 8:45–2:45
Morro Jable
➕ 165 F1 ✉ Morro Jable, on the beach just off the promenade
🕐 10–2:30

Where to...
Eat and Drink

Prices

Expect to pay for a three-course meal for one, excluding drinks and service

€ under €15   €€ €15-25   €€€ over €25

LA LAJITA

La Lajita Oasis Park €€

Oasis Park features three rustic restaurants decorated with greenery and rural bygones. The one by the main entrance backs onto exotic birdcages so their cries and calls make you feel as if you are eating in the jungle! (The other two are equally attractive and atmospheric but are only open to ticket holders.) It specialises in goat so try the fried goats' cheese in breadcrumbs with *membrillo* (quince) jelly and then move onto goat stew, perhaps finishing with *frangollo* and ice cream.

🕂 164 B3 ⌂ Carretera General de Jandia (FV-2 km 57.4)
☎ 928 161 135 ⏰ Daily 8-5 (meals served from noon onwards)

LA PARED

El Camello €€€

This gorgeous Andalusia-style hacienda is one of the most attractive restaurants in the whole of the island. Its rustic time-worn appearance is deceptive, as it was only built in the last decade. There is a lovely garden and courtyard with tiled benches where you can snack on tapas, and the main dining area is

straight from the pages of an interior design magazine, with pastel-washed walls, terracotta floors, tasteful chintzy soft furnishings and modern artworks. The changing international menu might include *crab au gratin* with saffron sauce, tatar of salmon with potato pancakes, anglerfish medallions in vegetable and mustard sauce as well as a hearty range of meat dishes. Finish off with fried ice cream in vanilla sauce. Excellent wine list, all ingredients are fresh, very good value. Reservations recommended.

🕂 164 B3 ⌂ Turn right on entering La Pared and follow the signs
☎ 928 549 090
⏰ Tue-Sun 1-11

Bahía La Pared €€

This beachside fish restaurant enjoys tremendous views and is very popular with locals and families, not least because there's a play area for children including a small pool with waterslides. The food is also excellent. If you're not sure which fish to choose ask the waiter for a recommendation. Book a table on the terrace, get here early evening and watch the sunset.

🕂 164 B3 ⌂ Playas de la Pared
☎ 928 549 030
⏰ Daily noon-10

COSTA CALMA

Copa €€-€€€

You're sure of a cheerful welcome in this bright and friendly modern German-owned restaurant run by Conny and Paul. The kitchen style is Erlebniskuche (creative cooking), drawing on a mix of Canarian and European influences. For example, starters include dates with bacon baked in mustard sauce, chicken fillets with curry prawns, *zarzuela* (a tomato-based stew) of vegetables, duck breast in calvados or rump steak Fuerteventura-style filled with goats' cheese. In the unlikely event that you can't see anything you like ask for the *tagesmenu* (daily specials). There are only a few tables so it's advisable to book.

164 B2 ⊠ **Behind CC El Palmeral (left-hand side)** ☎ **646 755 305**
🕔 **Tue–Sun 6pm–midnight**

Fuerte Action €–€€

Hang out with the local surf dudes and beautiful people at this friendly relaxed trendy modern café. MTV and surfing action plays on the screens but if that's not your thing you can easily escape on the terrace. Superior "fast foods" (spare ribs, chicken, pasta and home-made burgers), tapas, *bocadillos* (baguettes), a salad bar, good breakfasts, excellent coffee, juices, shakes and a mini-ice-cream parlour keep a broad range of customers coming back for more.

164 B2 ⊠ **CC El Palmeral (on main road next to petrol station)** ☎ **928 875 996** 🕔 **Daily 8am–12:30am (last meals 10:30pm)**

Posada San Borondon I €€

This dark ancient-looking low-ceilinged wooden Spanish tavern bar is decorated with apple presses, huge barrels and earthenware jars and just drips with old-world atmosphere. Being in Costa Calma it's all fake of course, but no less enjoyable for that. The cheerful owner theatrically pours Sangria from a great height and dispenses free *croquetas* (croquettes) and other nibbles to a mixed lively cosmopolitan crowd who enjoy the live Spanish music (every night except Monday). There is a long and interesting menu of mainland and islands tapas (for example, Asturian beans, mushrooms in sherry, Lanzarote-style lentils) and a shorter menu of simple Spanish-influenced meals; try the Moroccan kebab with spices from Ceuta or veal fillet in black pepper sauce. Highly recommended.

164 B2 ⊠ **CC Sotavento** ☎ **928 547 100** 🕔 **Daily 11am–1:30am**

La Terraza del Gato €€

The Risco del Gato is Costa Calma's most individual and unusual hotel (▶ 103) and this classy modern white café-restaurant reflects its sense of minimalist style. From its international dishes you might choose chicken yakitori or breast of duck with port and grapes; from Spain there are lamb cutlets from Burgos, asparagus from Navarra, carpaccio with manchego cheese, a wide range of cold meats and sausages, plus Canarian favourites too. Snacks are very reasonably priced. Chill out on the terrace in a comfy cane chair and enjoy a sea view. Live music Thursday and Sunday.

164 B2 ⊠ **Calle Sicasumbre** ☎ **928 547 030** 🕔 **Daily 12–12**

ESQUINZO

Marabú €€

One of the most frequently recommended restaurants in the south, the family-run Marabú ("Feathers"), is tucked away between the main road and the beach of Esquinzo in a charming garden terrace courtyard in a modern development. The interior boasts many traditional elements yet is also light, modern and inviting. Chef Ralf Johmann brings many years of international experience to such dishes as chateaubriand, grilled stingray with garlic and green peppers, sea bream in salt crust and milk lamb specialities. Holidaymakers and well-heeled locals rub shoulders here. Reservations recommended.

164 A1 ⊠ **Calle Fuente de Hija** ☎ **928 544 098, www.marabu-online.com** 🕔 **Mon–Sat 1–11**

JANDIA PLAYA

La Casa Vieja de Don Camillo €€

This is one of the few traditional restaurants in Jandia Playa. A typically Spanish bodega, it has a large terrace looking onto the main road but the best and quietest part of the restaurant is tucked away at the back. Hearty meat grills are the speciality of the house.

164 A1 ⊠ **Avenida del Saladar** ☎ **928 541 825** 🕔 **Daily noon–11**

Cervecería Olimpico €

This popular place is a clever mix of old-fashioned beer hall and 21st-century café, with floor to ceiling glass windows and a large attractive terrace where you can sit in comfy cane chairs looking across to the lighthouse. It has a wide selection of Spanish and German beers and an extensive range of other alcoholic drinks. At night the music is pumped up and it becomes a disco bar.

🔂 164 A1 🖂 Avenida del Saladar 🕿 928 166 012 🕑 Daily 10am–1am

Hong Kong €–€€

One of the best ethnic restaurants in the south, the authentic Chinese food at Hong Kong is ideal when you fancy a change from Canarian and Spanish cuisine. The chefs guarantee fresh fish and vegetables here so you may wish to add them to your choice of dishes, which in any case should include the house speciality, duck.

🔂 164 A1 🖂 Cosmo Shopping Centre 🕿 928 540 827 🕑 Daily 12–12

MORRO JABLE

Cofradía de Pescadores €

It's an experience to muck in with the local fishermen down at the port in their canteen bar, but actually more comfortable to sit outside where you can escape the TV and cigarette smoke and watch the boats. There's no frills and not a lot of choice – typically fish of the day, salad and potatoes, including the Canarian speciality of *papas arrugadas* – but quality and freshness is guaranteed, and, after all, if it's good enough for them...

🔂 165 F1 🖂 Calle El Muelle 🕿 928 540 179 🕑 Wed–Mon 8–5

Coronado €€€

One of the smartest and trendiest restaurants in the region, with a designer building, with a swimming pool and tennis courts open to guests, Coronado is ideal for a full meal or snack with a wide range of varying separate menus to suit every occasion; Bar Lounge Classics (meals to share, including paella and fondues); Appetisers and Tapas; Soups and Salads; Steaks; Seafood. Make room for the Postres (desserts)! Irresistible! The cuisine is of a very high standard and includes Thai, French, Italian and Spanish dishes. Occasional live music and shows.

🔂 165 F1 🖂 Calle El Sol, 14 🕿 928 541 174, www.restaurantecoronado.com

Posada San Borondon II €

Tucked away at the back of the ever-lively main square for restaurants, this dark single-storey colonial-style building hangs heavy with hams and garlic, agricultural implements and atmosphere. Yet, as at Posada San Borondon I (▶ 101), things are not what they seem. Although it is not at least a century old it was built around a decade ago. A menu of around 20 tapas is on offer, with live music most nights. A perfect place to start and end the evening. Friendly owner.

Saavedra Clavijo €€–€€€

This long-established restaurant is the most popular choice for fish in the old town. There is nearly always a buzz. Simply choose from the fresh fish display or ask the waiter for his recommendation.

🔂 165 F1 🖂 Avenida Tomás Grau Gurrea 🕿 928 166 080 🕑 Mon–Sat noon–late

Vesubio €–€€

Vesubio has a perfect people-watching location on the beach promenade just off the main square. Its menu wanders from island specials such as rabbit stew through 17 types of pizza and pasta respectively, or you could pick from the fresh fish display. If in doubt, go for a pizza.

🔂 165 F1 🖂 Avenida Tomás Grau Gurrea 🕿 928 540 391 🕑 Daily 11–10:30

🔂 165 F1 🖂 Peatonal La Piragua ("The Square") 🕿 928 541 428 🕑 Daily noon–late

Where to...
Stay

Prices

Expect to pay per double room, per night

€ under €60   €€ €60–90   €€€ €91–120   €€€€ over €120

JANDÍA PLAYA

Faro Jandía €€€

Standing opposite the landmark *faro* (lighthouse) and set back amid cheap shopping centres, this 4-star hotel is built in an attractive modern-local style and offers 214 spacious rooms to a mainly package-tour clientele of mixed nationalities. Nightly evening entertainment, three artificial grass tennis courts and the free use of a neighbouring Spa and Wellness Centre help to make this one of the resort's most popular hotels.

🚹 164 A1 ✉ Jandía Playa
☎ 902 300 363, www.farojandia.com

Iberostar Fuerteventura Park €€€–€€€€

This new hotel is located on the main Jandía beach with bright pastel-coloured single-room studio apartments or one/two-bedroom apartments. Breakfast only, half-board and all-inclusive tariffs are available. Sports facilities are limited with one tennis court and one multi-purpose court. The hotel's forte is its Thai Zen Space caring for body, mind and spirit, drawing on techniques dating back millennia.

🚹 164 A1 ✉ Pasaje Playa 3, Las
Gaviotas ☎ 922 070 300 (bookings) or
928 545 150, www.iberostar.com

Robinson Club Jandía Playa €€€€

Established in 1970, this was the famous German club's first ever venture and the first club-resort complex of its kind on the island. In those days it was very remote, but today its pioneering spirit might seem rather out of place amid the high rises and amusement arcades. It was completely renovated in 1998, has always had access to one of the best stretches of the Playa Matorral and continues to offer a very high level of comfort, facilities and entertainment. The resort is renowned for its excellent sports and water sports programmes. Facilities include 10 tennis courts, 40 top-quality windsurf boards and rigs, nine Hobie Catamarans and a diving school. There is another, much larger, Robinson Club nearby, at Esquinzo.

🚹 164 A1 ✉ Jandía Playa
☎ 928 169 100, in Germany 01803 76
24 67, www.robinson.de

COSTA CALMA

Bungalows Risco del Gato €€€€

One of the pioneers of the south, today the Risco del Gato 4-star luxury suite hotel is jostled by high-rise neighbours but remains unequalled for style and class. Its extraordinary white bungalows, which the architect intended to represent North African houses, look more like a sci-fi vision of how man might live in the future. Each comprises a conventionally housed bedroom, a round pod-like bathroom – featuring a large porthole window (each suite has its own private patio) – and a hemispherical ("half-pod") salon looking onto the gardens. It could look kitsch but remarkably it seems as cutting edge now as it must have done when it first opened in the late 1970s. There are two pools on different levels and the beautifully landscaped grounds provide a real feeling of space for its 107 guests. A spa and fitness centre, gym and gourmet restaurant look after its well-heeled Spanish and German clientele.

Rio Calma €€€€

Set high on a hill to the north, overlooking the whole resort, at first glance this building resembles a large church with a Victorian greenhouse attached. Walk though its doors and you enter a huge mock-medieval space. A glass lift in the shape of a fairy-tale castle turret takes you to the accommodation area and now you are in colonial Spain, with pastel-washed colonnaded streets and houses. It could be the Gothic quarter of Barcelona or perhaps Toledo, and its glorious gardens front onto a cliff top. In fact it's all completely new, the "church" included, and is the spectacular setting for one of the island's most luxurious hotels. All 384 rooms have stunning sea views and enjoy every facility, including spa, gourmet restaurants, four pools, tennis courts, pitch and putt, mini-golf and a professional entertainment programme that makes you never want to stray outside.

164 B2 Calle Sicasumbre 2
928 547175,
www.hotelriscodelgato.com

164 B2 El Granillo
928 876 149, www.r2hotels.com

ESQUINZO

Jandia Princess €€€€

This large white landmark hotel is built in traditional Canarian style. There are 528 stylish bedrooms set in blocks that rise to three storeys high and look onto landscaped gardens, three large pools – one heated – and the beautiful and relatively quiet beach of Playa Butihondo.

164 A1 Urb. Esquinzo Butihondo
928 544 089, 902 406 306
www.princess-hotels.com

MORRO JABLE

Riu Calypso €€€

Built on a hill on the front line of the most attractive part of the Jandia Playa/Morro Jable beach – just a short walk from Morro Jable centre – the view from the terraces of this hotel are probably the best in the resort. The pool area is attractive and if the rooms and dining areas are a little plain that is reflected in the very reasonable tariff. There is a Health and Wellness Centre (additional charge), a large swimming pool and a small children's pool.

165 F1 Playa de Jandia 928 546 306, 928 540 026, www.riu.com

PLAYA BARCA

Club Aldiana €€€€

Renowned for its extensive sports, spa and wellness facilities, the German-run Club Aldiana is one of the pioneers of this region, arriving here in the late 1970s. It is set in attractive grounds that tumble down to a beautiful stretch of beach where there is a diving school, and a fish restaurant that is indistinguishable from the genuine Canarian article. Most of its bungalows are fairly simple though there are a handful of newer luxury accommodations too.

164 A1 Jandia Playa
01803/901048 (9 cents/minute)
www.aldiana.de

Meliá Gorriones €€€–€€€€

Now fully renovated, this hotel stands in pole position and glorious isolation at the start of the most famous stretch of the Jandia beaches. The long-established Sol Gorriones has been one of the south's most famous and favourite hotels for several years and many people come here for the peace and quiet it offers. Its facilities are excellent, and the extensive mature grounds include four pools, one tennis court, a health centre and a gym. The famous Pro Centre René Egli Windsurf School (▶ 106) is also based here. Staff are very helpful and the first row of Casas del Mar apartments, built in 2000, offer great comfort and wonderful views.

164 A1 Playa Barca
928 547 025 (from Germany: 0800 14 14 444), www.solmelia.com

Where to...
Shop

JANDIA PLAYA

Most of the south's shopping opportunities are confined to the shopping centres of Jandía Playa and Costa Calma. The former is limited to cheap souvenirs, jewellers, perfume shops, duty-free electronics shops and "shoe bazaars" where you are expected to haggle over the price of footwear. The CC Cosmo (the last one on the main road heading to Morro Jable) is the best of the bunch, with its Juwelier Continental featuring brand names such as Swatch, Omega, Gucci, Tag Heuer, Longines, Breitling and Näo porcelain. There's a good perfume shop opposite with keen prices.

The island's weekly market sets out its stalls next door to the Cosmo every Thursday and at Costa Calma on Sunday morning.

COSTA CALMA

Costa Calma has more shopping centres than Jandía Playa though few of these offer little that is different or original. The best is the El Palmeral, on the main road by the filling station.

If you want to see what the well-heeled surf dude is wearing then pop into Fuerte Action, which has some of the most stylish surf clothes and accessories on the island. This brand is the brainchild of René Egli, who owns a water sports centre (▶ 106), so everything here is designed to be functional as well as fashionable. It's not cheap but it is high quality. Next door Hodge Podge also has some good surfing gear.

Inside the shopping centre, Mystic is good for aloe vera products and a small range of handicrafts. Based on a similar philosophy of natural products and handicrafts, The Earth Collection is worth a browse for island-sourced gifts and souvenirs.

The jewellery at First One, here prices range from pocket money to serious euros, is among the best on the entire island. (They also have a branch in the LTI Esquinzo Beach Hotel at Urb. Esquinzo Butihondo.)

Fuerte Cabrito sells clothes and accessories stylishly branded with the ubiquitous Fuerte goat logo (branches also in Morro Jable and Costa Calma) while Que Pasa offers stylish women's clothes and accessories; for details of both, visit www.cabrito-fuerteventura.com.

If you would like some Canarian flowers for the table at home then pop into Strelitzias at the Centro Commercial Costa Calma and they will pack these specially to be stowed in the aircraft hold. Also here is Maxoilores, one of the few shops (surprisingly) that sells kites and "wind toys".

MORRO JABLE

The old part of Morro Jable has a few shops of interest. Next to the square that holds the cafés, bars and restaurants, on Calle Nuestra Señora del Carmen, you will find Fuerte Cabrito and Que Pasa (see above), and just up from the square, on Calle Diputado Manuel Velázquez Cabrera, Fuertino sells high-quality children's clothes and toys bearing the favourite brand-name characters from Universal Studios, Disney Classics and such like. Walk along the promenade and you will find a shop/information centre devoted solely to aloe vera products.

LA LAJITA OASIS PARK

The shop at La Lajita Oasis Park sells a wide range of home accessories and unusual gifts. It's almost worth stopping just to look in the shop (no admission charge).

Where to...
Be Entertained

NIGHTLIFE

Most of the nightlife in this part of the island is confined to the large hotels and resort club complexes. Jandía Playa is the liveliest place with a number of disco bars. On summer weekends try the Discothek Stella at the Stella Canaris Hotel, the Disco Pub Tequila in the CC Faro or the Cervecería Olímpico on the seafront.

Costa Calma, true to its name, is generally quiet after dark though you might like to try the PMP disco-pub at the CC Cañada del Río, or the Eastside nightclub at the Sotavento Beach Club, Avenida Jahn Reisen. Fuerte Action (▲ 101), is generally lively. On the other side of the road in Costa Calma, the San Borondon I (▲ 101) is not only a good place to eat but has live music nightly.

WATER SPORTS

The Pro Centre René Egli, based at Sotavento Beach, is one of Europe's top centres for windsurfing and kiteboarding and the Windsurfing World Cup is held here in July (▲ 12). It is an excellent venue for just getting started or for polishing up your technique. Their expert coaches come from all over the world. The Fanatic windsurfing centre on Costa Calma beach is also recommended. Water sports facilities and instruction is highly rated at the club holiday village complexes of Club Robinson (▲ 103) and Aldiana (▲ 104) though these are only open to guests. For diving try the Sotavento Beach Club at Costa Calma (tel: 928 547 060), or the Felix Barakuda Club at Jandía Playa (tel: 928 541 418, www.tauchen-fuerteventura.com).

Jet Ski Safari-Excursions (tel: 616 437 184) at Jandía Playa is the place for jet skis, waterskiing, wakeboarding and water bananas. Tarajalejo is home to Cat Company (tel: 695 205 525, www.catmaran-segeln.de), the island's top catamaran operator.

OTHER SPORTS

The Academia de Golf Fuerteventura at La Pared is a curious sight with its white-ringed target-like greens set amid black ash "fairways". It's a challenge for non-regular golfers and useful short game practice for more experienced players. They have a putting green and a driving range and the friendly German owner (who speaks impeccable English) offers tuition (open Tue–Sat 10–6, Sun 10–2; tel: 928 549 105, www.golf-fuerteventura.net).

Tennis Matchpoint (tel: 639 313 664 or 609 236 257, www.tennis-matchpoint.de) is an enterprising company with seven German tennis coaches (English spoken) who offer tuition and put you together with players of similar ability to make up tournaments which are staged on the artificial grass courts at ten of the south's leading hotels. You can also hire courts and rackets from them.

EXCURSIONS

If you would like to look beneath the waves the Subcat, a twin-hulled submarine also based at Morro Jable will take you 30m (100 feet) down. (Trips run daily; €55 adults and €31 children (2–12 years), tel: 900 507 006, 629 153 583, www.subcat-fuerteventura.com).

Numerous deep-sea and big-game fishing trips depart from Morro Jable harbour and if you are in a group it might be worth chartering your own yacht for the day. The Magic Cat catamaran sails from Morro Jable (tel: 619 406 904).

Gran Canaria

Finding Your Feet 128 – 129
Getting Your Bearings 130 – 131
Don't Miss 132 – 133
At Your Leisure 134
Where to… 135 – 136

Gran Canaria
Finding Your Feet

Flights from Fuerteventura

Inter-island flights are operated by Binter Canarias. There is a 30-minute check-in time and the flight time is 40 minutes. The journey from the airport to Las Palmas takes around 30 minutes, so you can catch the 8am flight from Fuerteventura and be in Las Palmas before 10am. A one-way fare costs from around €64 (excl tax).

To book flights go to any travel agent, call 0034 902 391 392 or see www.bintercanarias.com

The first plane departs daily at 8am, and subsequent flights leave at regular intervals throughout the day. The last flights back from Gran Canaria are at 9:30pm (daily). This schedule is subject to change so check the timetable on the website. By catching the first and last flights you can spend at least ten hours in Las Palmas (pictured below and right).

You must reserve your seats as far ahead as possible as the planes are small and the early flights will be in demand by business people.

Arriving at Gando Airport

The Aeropuerto de Gando is 22km (14 miles) south of Las Palmas. The quickest but most expensive option is to take a taxi from outside the airport building. The journey time is around 20 minutes.

There is also a frequent reliable and inexpensive bus service to the capital. Bus 60 leaves from outside the airport terminal every 30 minutes from 6:30am to 9pm and then hourly until 2am. The journey takes around 30 minutes and arrives at the central bus station beside Parque de San Telmo in the heart of the city.

Tourist information offices

The main office (tel: 928 219 600, www.grancanaria.com; open Mon–Fri 8–3) is at Calle León y Castillo 17, near the bus station.

There is also an office at the airport at Arrivals Hall Gate A. They can help with overnight accommodation.

There are information kiosks in Plaza de Hurtado Mendoza (open Mon–Fri 10–7:30, Sat 10–3); Avenida José Mesa y López (open Mon–Fri 10–3:30); Paseo de las Canteras (open Mon–Fri 10–7:30, Sat 10–3); and Parque de San Telmo (open Mon–Fri 10–7:30, Sat 10–3).

If you want to check out what is going on in Las Palmas before you get there, see the official website above or www.promocionlaspalmas.com (Spanish only). These will also give you details of the city's famous Carnival celebrations.

Getting around
City buses
If you are only here for the day the most useful bus is No1 which runs between the old town (Parque de San Telmo) and the port (Parque de Santa Catalina).

The *Guagua Turística* (Tourist Bus) is a hop-on/hop-off tour bus that makes a two-hour circuit of the city beginning and ending in Parque de Santa Catalina (www.guaguas.com/turistica.htm). Tickets cost €8 and are valid for the day. The bus leave Parque de Santa Catalina every half-hour from 9:30am–5:45pm. You can also pick up the bus from outside the central bus station at Parque de San Telmo.

Taxis
These operate as on Fuerteventura (➤ 37) and fares are very similar. For local journeys all fares are metered.

When to come
Avoid Monday when several attractions are closed and Sunday when the market and many shops are closed. If you want to see the excellent folk dancing at the Pueblo Canario (pictured on page 127 and below) come on Thursday.

Carnaval (February) can be a great time to come as the celebrations here are massive compared to those on Fuerteventura. Do stay overnight, however, or the party will be just beginning when it is time for you to fly back!

Flights, sailings and accommodation are at a real premium during *Carnaval* so you will need to book well ahead.

Timing it right
Many shops close for lunch between 1:30pm and 4:30pm though department stores and malls remain open throughout the day.

Getting Your Bearings

Cosmopolitan, buzzing with locals going about their daily business, teeming with shops, restaurants and a vibrant cultural life, Las Palmas is a real contrast to the wild landscapes of Fuerteventura. Whether you arrive by bus or by boat, the *Guagua Turística* (Tourist Bus) is perfectly placed to whisk you round the sights and shops of this exciting city.

Las Palmas stretches out like a long thin lizard along the island's northeastern tip. The shape of the city has the effect of making it seem larger than it is. In fact, from Parque de Santa Catalina to Parque de San Telmo – the two reference points that will be of most use to day trippers – is around 3.5km (2 miles).

The oldest part of town is the Vegueta District, around 800m (880 yards) south of Parque de San Telmo, with cobbled streets, shady squares and colonial-style architecture. It was founded by the island conqueror Juan Rejón in 1478 on a *vegueta* (meadow). Between Vegueta and Parque de San Telmo is Triana, an attractive mix of buildings spanning the 16th to 20th centuries. Here you will find lively shopping streets and open-air bars.

The area between Parque de San Telmo and Parque de Santa Catalina is residential, with the Pueblo Canario being the only point of visitor interest. Santa Catalina is the hub of the modern city and Playa de las Canteras, one of the finest city beaches in the world, is just a short walk away. Beyond the port, Puerto de la Luz, which is Spain's largest, the volcanic peaks of La Isleta provide a scenic backdrop.

Take in the colonial architecture in Plaza de Santa María and Triana

★ **Don't Miss**

1 Casa de Colón
➤ 132

2 Museo Canario
➤ 133

At Your Leisure

3 Mercado de Vegueta ➤ 134

4 Catedral de Santa Ana ➤ 134

5 Museo Pueblo Canario ➤ 134

❶Casa de Colón

There is no proof that Christopher Columbus (Cristobal Colón in Spanish) ever stayed at this beautiful old house, but it is widely agreed that he did call at Las Palmas on the voyage that led to the "discovery" of the New World in 1492, and it is almost certain that he would have been offered accommodation here.

The Casa de Colón was originally the military governor's residence, one of the first buildings to be completed in Las Palmas following the Spanish conquest of 1478. It is a magnificent example of traditional Canarian colonial architecture, with carved stone portals, dark wooden balconies and richly ornamented facades.

The splendid stone portals of the Casa de Colón

Today it is a museum dedicated to the explorer and his famous voyages.

If time is tight, concentrate on the ground-floor rooms as they offer the most interesting exhibits. Among the charts, navigational instruments and model boats, you will find a reconstruction of Columbus's cabin on board the *Santa María*; the log book of his first voyage to the New World; the seals of the Treaty of Tordesillas (1494), which carved the Atlantic into Spanish and Portuguese spheres of influence; and the map of the known world in 1500 by a cartographer who accompanied Columbus. The only thing missing is any personal possessions of Columbus himself.

The crypt is devoted to objects from the pre-Columbian period (ie, before 1492) and shows the richness of the native American cultures.

➕ 169 C1 ✉ Calle Colón 1 ☎ 928 312 373, www.grancanariacultura.com (Spanish only) 🕐 Mon–Fri 9–7 Sat–Sun 9–3 💶 Free

2 Museo Canario

This excellent museum is home to the archipelago's most comprehensive collection on the culture and lifestyle of the aboriginal Canarians known as the Guanches. You can see everything in around an hour.

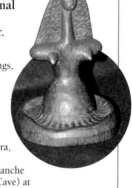

The first three rooms are devoted to Guanche dwellings, agriculture and economy. If you are in a hurry, move swiftly through these to room four, the magic and religion gallery which contain original Guanche fertility idols, unmissable on account of their exaggerated genitalia (you will doubtless have seen some of these in the shops in Fuerteventura in reproduction form). The best known is the Idol of Tara, possibly symbolising the earth goddess.

Here also is a reproduction of the most famous Guanche dwelling yet discovered, the *Cueva Pintada* (Painted Cave) at Galdár on Gran Canaria plus a large collection of original *pintaderas* (wooden identity stamps), which again you will probably have seen on sale in reproduction form.

The most compelling sections of the museum are rooms six to nine, which deal with death and mummification – a practice that the Guanches probably learned from the Egyptians. Some of the mummies are over 1.8m (6ft) high, showing that the Guanches were a tall race. There are also many skulls that have been trepanned, a surgical operation in which holes or incisions were made in the skull of a living person, possibly in the hope of gaining spiritual enlightenment or for other mystical purposes.

The captions are all in Spanish, but the museum sells a guidebook with English and German translations.

A fertility artefact (top) from the Museo Canario (bottom)

➕ 169 C1 ✉ Calle Dr Verneau 2
☎ 928 336 800,
www.elmuseocanario.com
🕐 Mon–Fri 10–8, Sat–Sun 10–2
💲 Moderate

At Your Leisure

The cathedral interior is full of light and space and grand bishops' tombs. A separate ticket gives access to the cathedral tower.

🚼 169 C1 ⊠ Plaza de Santa Ana (entrance on Calle Espirito Santo) ☎ 928 313 600 🕓 Outside of service times (daily 8–10), when entry to the cathedral is free, buy a ticket at the Museo Diocesano next door, (Mon–Thu 10–4, Fri–Sat 10–1pm 🎫 Inexpensive

🟥 Museo Pueblo Canario

This charming "village" of traditional Canarian buildings may seem like a tourist gimmick but it was designed as a serious attempt to preserve Canarian culture from the threat of mass tourism. The folk dancing is excellent but takes place only on Sundays at 11:30am. There are also shops, a café, a restaurant and the Museo Néstor, dedicated to the *moderniste* artist Nestor Fernandez de la Torre who created the village with his brother Miguel in the 1930s.

🚼 169 B3 ⊠ Parque Doramas ☎ 928 242 985, Museum 928 245 135, www.museonestor.com 🕓 Tue–Sat 10–8, Sun 10:30–2:30 (Museum Tue–Fri 10–8, Sun 10:30–2:30) 🎫 Free (Museum inexpensive)

🟥 Mercado de Vegueta

The oldest, most colourful and most comprehensive market in the city (established 1854), this is where the locals come to buy a cornucopian range of fish, fruit, vegetables and cheese. Around the market are tapas bars and *churrerías* where people come to buy their *churros* (extruded dough fritters), which they dunk into cups of thick hot chocolate.

🚼 169 C1 ⊠ Plaza del Mercado/Calle Mendizábal 🕓 Mon–Thu 6–2, Fri–Sat 6–3

🟥 Catedral de Santa Ana

The largest church in the Canary Islands dominates the Vegueta skyline. Begun in 1497 it took over 400 years to complete and so is a curious mix of Gothic, Renaissance, baroque and neo-Classical styles.

In its courtyard, replete with orange trees, is a beautiful cloister built in the late 16th century with wooden galleries along two sides. A staircase leads to the chapter house, which has a handmade ceramic tile floor unique in the archipelago.

Park life

Parque de San Telmo is the prettiest of the city parks and features a bandstand and a much-photographed *moderniste* (Spanish art nouveau) café inside a pavilion decorated with ceramic tiles. Parque de Santa Catalina is the throbbing hub of the city with cafés, newsstands, shops and the Museo Elder science museum. Tourists mingle with sailors, shoeshine boys, hustlers and African traders while old men play dominoes and chess beneath the palm trees.

Where to...
Eat and Drink

Prices
Expect to pay for a three-course meal for one, excluding drinks and service
€ under €15 **€€** €15–25 **€€€** over €25

Most restaurants open throughout the year, though some take an annual holiday in August.

Café Santa Catalina €
This pleasant open-air cafe with a shady terrace beneath the palms is where the old locals gather to play chess and dominoes. The lunch menu is mostly standard fare such as pizzas and pastas but at any time it is an ideal place for an ice cream or a coffee and pastry.

✚ 169 A5 ☒ Parque Santa Catalina
🕒 Daily 10am–1am

Casa Carmelo €€–€€€
Renowned for the high quality of its grilled meats (particularly steak) and fish, and its special sauce, this traditional restaurant is popular with foreign visitors who also come to enjoy the great views across the beach.

✚ 169 A5 ☒ Paseo de las Canteras, 2 ☎ 928 469 056
🕒 Daily 1:30–4:30, 7:30–11:30

Casa Montesdeoca €€€
Close to the Casa Colón, this is the city's most elegant restaurant, situated in a 16th-century town house. You can just have a drink here but booking a table on the patio beneath the palms is

something special. The service is very formal and the cooking is first class, featuring Canarian and Spanish dishes with the emphasis on fish.

✚ 169 C1 ☒ Calle Montesdeoca 10
☎ 928 333 466 🕒 Mon–Sat 1–4, 8–11:30

Don Quijote II €€
Unwind from a shopping trip at this do-it-yourself restaurant where the speciality is *carne a la piedra* (steak, chicken or pork, cooked at the table on a hot stone). It comes with French fries, a big bowl of salad and a selection of relishes.

✚ 169 A4 ☒ Calle Secretario Artiles 74 ☎ 928 272 786
🕒 Daily 1–4, 8–midnight

Hipócrates €€
This place is a treat for vegetarians, serving organic meat-free cuisine in a town house opposite the Casa de Colón. The salads are works of art, piled high with tropical fruits, which also feature strongly in the desserts. There is a good selection of herbal

teas and fresh fruit juices. The décor is bright and airy.

Hotel Madrid €
Enjoy an early evening or lunchtime drink and tapas outside this historic hotel – Franco spent a last night of peace here in 1936 on the eve of the Spanish Civil War – set on one of the nicest squares in the city. The bar also serves reasonably priced set meals.

✚ 169 C1 ☒ Plaza de Cairasco 4
☎ 928 360 664 🕒 Daily 10am–1am

O'Sole Mio €–€€
On one of the city's most beautiful squares, this Triana pizzeria buzzes. Pizzas are cooked in a wood-fired brick oven (try their non-traditional "African Pizzas" with exotic fruits) – steak, fish and pasta dishes are also on the menu.

✚ 169 C1 ☒ Plaza de Cairasco 3
☎ 928 383 746 🕒 Daily 1–4, 8–11

✚ 169 C1 ☒ Calle Colón 4
☎ 928 311 171 🕒 Mon 8:30 pm–midnight, Tue–Sat 1–4, 8:30–midnight, Sun 1–4

Where to...
Shop

Most shops are open Monday to Saturday 10am to 8pm, although some close for lunch between 1:30pm and 4:30pm; the department stores open from 10am to 10pm.

Avenida Mesa y López

A five-minute walk south of Parque Santa Catalina, this is the main shopping street with two branches of Spain's most famous department store, El Corte Inglés, opposite each other. The main store has four floors of fashions and the Club del Gourmet features Canarian and Spanish food and wines. The top-floor café is a good place for a break. The second shop specialises in books, music, electronic goods, household items and souvenirs. It too features a good top-floor restaurant specialising in Canarian cuisine.

The rest of the Avenida is devoted to fashion and designer boutiques with famous international and top Spanish names.

Triana

If you would like to combine shopping with sightseeing and atmosphere head for Calle Mayor La Triana in the heart of the old city. Formerly the main shopping street, it features some beautiful architecture with many shops retaining their *moderniste* (Spanish art nouveau) shopfronts. There are a few big names here but it is the quirky arty, crafty shops in the side streets which give this area its appeal. Look out for Ezquerra (Calle Travieso) for hats, *mantillas* (shawls) and Canarian desert boots; Fedac (Calle Domingo J Navarro), a government-sponsored craft shop which sells a wide range of goods at very reasonable prices; Casa Ricardo (corner Calle Mayor and Calle Losero), the sweetshop of your childhood dreams; Atarecos (Calle Peregrina) for local handicrafts and Latin American clothing, Calle Peregrina also contains several antiques shops. On Calle Mayor is a branch of Natura Selection offering fair-trade goods and crafts from around the world.

The best time to visit this area is from 6pm onwards during the early evening *paseo* (promenade) when locals and tourists take to the streets and buskers come out to entertain.

Parque de Santa Catalina

The area around the park is something of an Oriental bazaar with numerous Asian-run shops selling cheap cameras, watches, cigars, clothes and electronic goods.

The main streets are Calle de Tomás Miller, Calle Luis Morote and Calle Alfredo L Jones. Haggling is the norm so be prepared. Prices are not necessarily any keener than on Fuerteventura but there is a much larger range of stock here.

Markets

For food of all kinds visit the Mercado de Vegueta (▶ 134). If you are here on a Sunday morning, visit the lively Rastro (flea market) at Parque de Santa Catalina, which attracts many African traders with their colourful merchandise. The Mercado de las Flores on the Plaza de Santo Domingo (just south of the Museo Canario in the old town) sells arts, crafts and, as you would expect, flowers.

Malls

The biggest mall near the centre of town is Las Arenas, at the west end of Playa de Las Canteras and close to one of the stops on the Guagua Turistica bus route.

Pueblo Canario

This complex of traditionally built island houses provides very pleasant relaxed surroundings in which to buy top-quality souvenirs, craft items, ceramics, books and Gran Canarian folk music (▶ 134).

Walks and Drives

1 Isla de Lobos 138 – 141
2 Sendero de Bayuyo Volcanoes
  142 – 144
3 Northern and Central Highlights
  145 – 149
4 Coast-to-Coast 150 – 152

1 Isla de Lobos

Walk

You will feel like a desert island explorer here. Lobos is a microcosm of "the mainland" with mini-volcanoes, small lagoons, a superb little beach, a tiny ramshackle fishing village, a picturesque lighthouse and mountaintop views that equal any on Fuerteventura. Choose a clear day to enjoy it. You need a modicum of fitness to climb the mountain; while boots are not necessary, sturdy trainers are a minimum requirement. ▶ 51–52 for more on the island.

Tip

There are rarely too many people "discovering" Lobos, but when you disembark let other island explorers go on ahead – that way you can have the island all to yourself, or at least it will feel that way!

DISTANCE 10km (6 miles) **TIME** 2 hrs 30 mins–3 hrs
START/END POINT El Muelle (the harbour) ✚ 163 E5

Getting to the start point

There are three boats that run daily to the island from Corralejo. If you want to eat on the island as well as fit in sunbathing, choose the service that gives you the most time. (For more details ▶ 52.)

1–2

On disembarking at El Muelle, turn right, following the signpost towards "El Puertito 7 mins" and "Las Lagunitas 18 mins". El Puertito ("the little port") is possibly the most tumbledown fishing village you will ever see, little more than a motley collection of a dozen or so wooden and stone shacks that have seen better days. Pass through (it doesn't take long!) and fork right to head to

After your walk round Isla de Lobos, relax!

Punta Martiño

③ ⌂ **Faro de Lobos**

the sea. The paths at this point are quite confusing (and after rain can also be soft and muddy) but fear not as you will soon join a proper track. At the edge of a small promontory you look out across to Lanzarote. To your left is Las Lagunitas ("the little lagoons"), a sandy salt marsh where migratory birds come to feed and rest. Walk across the sandy flats and rejoin the signposted pathway.

2–3

As you reach the end of the salt flats the path turns right towards the sea but this is no more than a short detour. Ignore it and keep going straight ahead following the trail up a slight incline to the left where it leads to what appears to be a small white tin shelter. In fact, as you get closer this turns out to be the underneath of an information board on the flora and fauna of Las Lagunitas. Look across the island and you can see right back to the dunes of Corralejo. A broad sandy path

Birdlife

Isle de Lobos is an Area of Special Protection for Birds. Look out for Cory's Shearwater (known locally as Pardela Cenicienta), a large gull with a slow, graceful flying action.

Roque Cercado
Ploya del Sobrado
59m ▲

Caleta del Palo

Punta Salidero

Morros de la Pila

Caldera de Lobos

127m ▲ (4)
Montaña de la Caldera

Los Toscones

Isla de Lobos

El Marrajo

Colorado
37m ▲

Morro de la Morada

51m ▲ Atalaya del Faro

Ploya de la Arena

Parque   Natural

Morro de las Lentejas

El Gigante

del   Islote

de   Lobos

Las Tres Hermanas

Las Lagunitas (2)
32m ▲

Punta Mantequilla

Roques del Puertito

EL PUERTITO

El Roque

Ploya de la Calera

El Muelle

(1) ★

Corralejo

Punta del Marrajo

Ploya de la Caleta

0 ⊢ 500 metres
0 ⊢ 500 yards

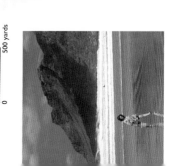

leads from here to the Faro de Lobos (lighthouse) and should take you another 25 to 30 minutes.

Just before you reach the Faro at Punta Martiño, the northernmost part of the island, you pass by a number of small brown protuberances, typically around 3–8m (10–26 feet) high. These are *hornitos* (literally "little ovens"), mini-volcanoes, formed not in the usual way, by magma pushing up the earth, but by steam-driven explosions (known technically as phreatic eruptions) that occur when water beneath the ground is heated by magma, lava, hot rocks or new volcanic activity. These were created some 8,000 years ago and are best appreciated from the lighthouse which sits on a large raised concrete base. From here there are also tremendous views across to Lanzarote. The resort of Playa Blanca and its Papagayo beaches are ahead of you and looming above them are the Montañas del Fuego (► 114–115), while to the right the metropolis of blurred white blocks is Puerto del Carmen.

Rejoin the path which turns almost back on itself at this point.

Catch the early boat out to the island

3–4

Continue on the broad sandy path for around 15 to 17 minutes. The Montaña de la Caldera looms large to your right but avoid the temptation to take the first turn off to the right, which in fact leads to Caleta del Palo (► next page). Take the next path right – the signpost on the main track says "Faro 20 mins, Muelle 19 mins" – and within 10m (11 yards) you will see another sign "Montaña de la Caldera 27 mins". This refers to the time it takes to reach the 127m-high (416

Top tips

Bring a sunshade, hat and plenty of water. The restaurant sells water and will make you a basic tuna *bocadillo* (baguette) but unless you have booked for lunch that's the top and bottom of the refreshment options. They do have ice creams but these are reserved for restaurant customers!

If it's a windy morning it may be best to give this trip a miss.

feet) summit. This is quite a steep climb so take it easy, particularly as the steps finish about three-quarters of the way up and the last part is a bit of a scramble. It's well worth the effort, however. The 360-degree views covering the three islands of Fuerteventura, Lanzarote and Lobos itself are exhilarating. The excursion boats and catamarans anchored off the white-sand bay to your left are a picture, while way down below, on the other side of the ridge, is the almost perfect semicircular stone beach of Caleta del Palo, right inside the mountain crater. You can quite safely walk a long way right along the ridge looking down onto Corralejo, though do take care if it's a windy day.

4–1

Descend the mountain and return to the main track. Turn right and it's a five-minute walk to the lovely little white sand crescent of Playa la Concha (also known as Playa de la Caleta). This is an ideal spot for family bathing, with very calm waters and a gently sloping sandy bottom. From here it's a three-minute stroll back to the harbour.

Taking a break

If you intend to eat at the island restaurant you MUST make a reservation as soon as you land. The restaurant is closed in the morning but just ask the people unloading food on the dockside about lunch and they will produce a book in which to write your name. Beware, however, that if you are going to take a leisurely walk around the island you may not get back until around 2pm (later if you spend a long time on the beach). This should still give you just enough time to eat but check what time they stop serving. There is no menu as such, but the choice is generally paella or fresh fish.

The views of Fuerteventura are spectacular

2 Sendero de Bayuyo Volcanoes

Walk

The Sendero de Bayuyo is the only marked countryside pathway on Fuerteventura (there is another on Isla de Lobos). It takes you past dramatic volcanic formations, shows the harsh conditions of goat herding and offers wonderful views to the north of the island and beyond.

DISTANCE 5km/3 miles (9km/5 miles if you continue on to Corralejo) **TIME** 2 hrs–2 hrs 30 mins

START/END POINT Just north of Lajares ✠ 163 D4

1–2

To find the start of the walk, take the FV109 to Lajares from Corralejo. Just before Lajares, opposite the Witchcraft Surf Shop (on the left), look to your right and you will see a curious purple-brown volcano with two depressions that resemble large eyes – this is where you are heading! To get there continue for 0.5km (550 yards) to the football ground and turn right just in front of it. Continue for 1km (0.6 mile) past a sign to the Zoo Safari Calderon Hondo (now closed down) and park past the last house on the right-hand side of the road. A path cobbled with rough black volcanic stones marks the way.

Follow the black brick road. The pock-marked volcano that you saw from the main road, the Montaña Colorada (Coloured Mountain), which rises to 240m (790 feet), should always be to your left. Look back and you can see the little white houses of Lajares. The path disappears briefly but veer to the right and you will soon pick it up again. Look out over the black *malpaís* (rough volcanic debris) to your right. *Malpaís* translates as "bad steps", which you will appreciate if you leave the path and try to traverse it (this is not recommended!). It was formed some 8,000 years ago and is speckled grey-green with lichen, a fungi which is a very good indicator of air pollution. As long as the air is pure the lichen will thrive.

After about 20 minutes of walking, the Montaña Colorada dips in a saddle and as you pass it

CORRALEJO

0   ½ mile

0   1 km

FV

you will see a large triangular footing with an "entrance" formed by two standing stones. Go through these and crest a small hill and some 6km (4 miles) to the northeast you can see the snow-white dunes of Corralejo (▶ 48–50).

FV101

Montaña San Rafael

271m
▲ Volcan de Bayuyo

Malpais de Bayuyo

248m Las Calderas

253m
▲ Caldera Encantada

233m
▲ Caldera de Rebanada

235m
▲

162m
▲ Calderón Hondo
278m

240m
▲ Montaña Colorada

④

③

②

①

Majanicho

LAJARES

FV109

You can see traditional windmills and a goat or two along the way

2–3

After around 30 minutes you will pass through a low drystone wall. Due north on the horizon is Playa Blanca, Lanzarote and its mountains. After another five to ten minutes the path forks. Go left and ignore the two smaller paths turning off to the right. After three to four minutes of steep climbing you will reach a viewing platform at an altitude of 278m (910 feet). This not only offers a wonderful panorama but also lets you peer right down into the extinct, perfectly round crater of the volcano. Look to your left and you will see a spectacular "cowl" that shows how the volcano collapsed. Down in the crater prickly pears are growing, while a family of goats often graze and laze right by the crater edge. You can skirt part of the crater lip but take care, and it is not recommended to try to walk right around it. The panorama in front of you

Time it right

Although this landscape is harsh and barren for much of the year, in spring there is a surprising amount of foliage around. Try to time the walk so that you end up as the sun is going down, when the volcanoes are tinged with purple and amber.

The route has views into the crater of Montaña Colorada and the white village of Majanicho

stretches from the little white fishing village of Majanicho to the west (left) to the distant white blur of Puerto del Carmen on Lanzarote to the east (right). Peer closely and just outside Majanicho you can see the outline of a new housing development. In the middle distance to the east stands the volcano of Bayuyo at 271m (889 feet).

3–4

Descend the path and take the second fork left to the goat herders' building that you could see from the top of Calderón Hondo. Look inside this primitive shelter (it is a replica purpose-built for visitors) and you will see its thatch and mud roof construction set on volcanic drystone walls. The small conical construction nearby shows how a primitive oven was fashioned. A corral has also been made from the volcanic debris.

4–1

At this point you can either head back the way you came or extend the walk by exploring the volcanoes that you have seen from your viewpoint. Use Bayuyo as your guide point, follow the path and in an hour or so you will be standing below it. If you want to climb the summit it takes around 30 minutes and offers

wonderful views down into Corralejo's "backyard". Corralejo itself is another hour or so walk away.

Taking a break

Take water with you on the trek. There are several good places in Lajares for lunch (▶ 60) or you could have a snack in the Witchcraft Surf Shop which serves drinks, cakes and sandwiches.

3 Northern and Central Highlights

Drive

This full-day drive will show you the best of north and central Fuerteventura. The roads are fast and straight in the north, often slow and tortuous in the heart of the island, but well worth the effort with magnificent mountain scenery.

DISTANCE 151km/94 miles (with options for short cuts) **TIME** Full day
START/END POINT Corralejo ➕ 163 E5

1–2

Begin in Corralejo (distances are taken from the roundabout by the football ground). After 1km (0.5 mile) go right at the next roundabout and take the FV101 to La Oliva. To your right is the **Volcan de Bayuyo**, rising to 271m (889 feet) (▶ 33).

After 13km (8 miles) you will pass through one of the island's best-kept villages, **Villaverde** (▶ 56). Two adjacent windmills form a backdrop and, as you are about to leave the village, note the **Hotel Rural Mahoh** (▶ 62), built in the vernacular style with immaculate gardens. Just before you reach the centre of **La Oliva** (▶ 53), notice the ruined Casa del Inglés to your right. A one-way system takes you round the right-hand side of the village centre, but as you pass the **Centro de Arte Canario** (▶ 53) look straight ahead to the perfectly triangular cone of Montaña de Frontón, which provides a spectacular backdrop.

Take in ruins, historical villages and spectacular scenery on this drive

Time it right

There are several museums and attractions on this route so if you want the option of visiting them it is best to avoid Mondays and Saturdays when most are closed. None of them are "must see", though the most interesting are the Ecomuseo de La Alcogida at Tefía and the Casa de Santa María at Betancuria.

2–3

Continue through the centre of La Oliva on the FV10 towards Puerto del Rosario and after 5km (3 miles) the sacred mountain of **Tindaya** (▶ 57) looms on your right. After another 2–3km (1–2 miles) look to your right and standing in front of the 399m-high

(1,309 feet) Montaña Quemada you will see what appears to be a tiny statue dwarfed by the mountain. It is in fact the 2.3m-high (7.5 feet) monument to **Miguel de Unamuno** (▶ 76). Shortly after this, turn right, onto the FV207. The road swoops down into a mostly empty valley with just a few homesteads amid the fields. After 7km (4 miles) you come to the little village of Tefia. Just as you leave the village there is a much-photographed **molina** to the right and after a few hundred metres on your left is the **Ecomuseo de La Alcogida** (▶ 74), usually with a pair of donkeys and a camel in a roadside field.

Taking a break

If you made a late start and fancy a fish lunch after passing through Tefia, take the turning right onto the FV221 and drive 11km (7 miles) to the pretty little port of Los Molinos (▶ 75) where there are two good seaside restaurants.

Don't miss the monument to Miguel de Unamuno

Half-day option

If the Ecomuseo de La Alcogida detains you and you want to turn this drive into a half-day tour, head back north from Tefia and turn right onto the FV10. Go through Tetir then, after around 15km (9 miles), just before the coast and the outskirts of Puerto del Rosario, follow the FV3 ring road to the left towards Corralejo. Then simply hug the coastline all the way back (some 35km/22 miles) to Corralejo.

3–4

Continue for 6km (4 miles) and turn right on the FV30 towards Betancuria. The road now starts to climb and the pretty little roadside hamlet of **Valle de Santa Inés**, with its Artesanía and Casa del Queso, is a "starter" for the

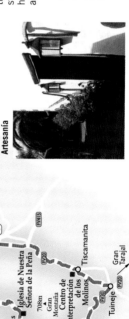

Visit the Centro de Artesanía

Taking a break

There are several refreshment options at Betancuria (►79). The Mirador Morro de Veloso also serves good food.

Puerto Lajas

El Time

PUERTO DEL ROSARIO

Miguel de Unamuno

Tetir

Casillas del Angel

Llano Pelado

Tefia

Ecomuseo de La Alcogida

La Ampuyenta

□ **Triquivijate**

Los Molinos

Valle de Santa Inés

Mirador de Morro Veloso

Centro de Artesanía Molino

Antigua

666m

Betancuria

Vega de Rio Palmas

Iglesia de Nuestra Señora de la Peña

708m ▲ Gran Montaña

Centro de Interpretación de los Molinos

Tiscamanita

Ajuy

Ermita de Virgen de la Peña

Embalse de las Peñitas

Pájara

Tuineje

Gran Tarajal

0   5 km
0   3 miles

The church in Pájara has a sandstone portal with unusual markings

"main course" of **Betancuria** (▶70–72). If you intend stopping in the old island capital (and it is highly recommended) it too has an Artesanía and Casa del Queso so there is no need to break your journey yet. After another 2km (1 mile) turn right towards Betancuria and the road winds tightly upwards. Look high above you and you can see what seems to be a large chalet-style building with picture windows. It is the **Mirador de Morro Veloso**. Stop here and admire the wonderful view north. (If for any reason the mirador is not open, there is a place where you can pull off the road almost adjacent to it and enjoy the same view).

4–5

The old capital of **Betancuria** is full of sightseeing interest and can easily occupy a half-day in its own right (▶70–72).
Continue through Betancuria glancing down below to your right just after you pass through the centre to see the roofless ruin of the Convent of San Buenaventura. As you leave Betancuria behind, palm trees are much in evidence on this stretch of road together with metal wind pumps, some of them dating back to the 1930s. After 5km (3 miles) you will pass the pretty little church of Vega de Río Palmas.

After another 1km (0.6 mile) or so there is a pull-off point on the right from which you can look down onto the Embalse de las Peñitas (reservoir). If it is dry it looks like a large brown field, though unnaturally straight and flat. Beside it, nestled in to the gully and just visible, is the ancient little white chapel of La Virgen de la Peña, the island's patron saint. The road winds upwards again, passing through mountains that resemble melted chocolate, and reaches one of the highlights of this tour, the Degollada de los Granadillos. Pull off the road to enjoy the spectacular views east and west; a stylised whitewashed portal, marking the provincial boundary, stands in stark relief to the dark brown mountain scenery and gives this pass even greater drama.
Continue onto Pájara staying on the FV30 towards Gran Tarajal.

5–6

After the barren mountains of the Betancuria province, pretty **Pájara** (▶78) is an oasis of colour. Park by the church and even if it is closed do have a look at its portal. Continue ahead with the church to your left. After 9km (6 miles) turn left at the town of Tuineje onto the FV20 towards Antigua and Puerto del Rosario. This is tomato-growing country and

Detour

Somewhat confusingly, 1km (0.5 mile) or so after the church of Vega de Río Palmas, another sign leads off right also to Vega de Río Palmas. This pleasant side road winds through palm groves and runs more or less parallel to the main road. It finishes in a dead end after around 3km (2 miles) overlooking the Embalse de las Peñitas (reservoir) (▶ above).

you will notice large polythene tomato tents dotted around the town. If the parish church is open, call in to see the altarpiece, which depicts the Battle of Tamasite in 1740, when the locals repelled a raid by British privateers.

Tiscamanita lies 4km (2.5 miles) north and its **Centro de Interpretación de los Molinos** (▶ 78) is just north of the centre. From here, the road to Antigua is straight and fast but enjoy the scenery to your left with mountains running along the spine of the island. Largest of all is the Gran Montaña, which at 708m (2,322 feet) is one of the island's highest peaks.

6–7

Stop off in the centre of the appealing old town of **Antigua**, have a look at the church (▶ 73) and then head north for 1–2km (0.6–1 mile) to reach the **Centro de Artesanía Molino** (▶ 73) with its landmark 200-year-old windmill. With its garden, plaza and large **rotunda restaurant** it's a good place for a break (▶ 79–80). After another

2–3km (1–2 miles) you will come to the small town of La Ampuyenta, home to the Casa-Museo Dr Mena, which is a fine example of a large, comfortable, upper-class country house dating from the 19th century (open Tue–Fri 9:30–3, Sun 9:30–5:30, inexpensive). The village's 17th-century Ermita de San Pedro de Alcántara chapel is also worth a look.

7–1

Continue on the FV20 towards Puerto del Rosario to Casillas del Ángel where the Iglesia de Santa Ana contains an 18th-century carving of St Anne. After 5km (3 miles) turn left at Llano Pelado onto the FV225. Fork off left after 2–3km (1–2 miles) and head towards Tetir. This pretty little village is worth a coffee stop before continuing on the FV10 through La Oliva and back north to Corralejo.

The short way back

Just north of La Ampuyenta you have the option of returning to Corralejo through Tefía. If you want to take this option, turn left on the FV30 towards Valle de Santa Inés, then right towards Tefía on the FV207.

Learn about the island's windpower at the Centro de Interpretación de los Molinos on the way

4 Coast-to-Coast

Walk

This easy walk crosses La Pared isthmus at its narrowest point. It's a mere 3km (2 miles) stroll from the manicured hotel grounds and shopping centres of Costa Calma to the wild windswept wave-beaten Barlovento coastline. This is a golden opportunity to see the beaches of the west without the need for a 4WD vehicle.

DISTANCE 10km (6 miles) **TIME** Around 3 hrs
START/END POINT Centro Commercial El Palmeral, Costa Calma ⊞ 164 B2

1–2

The track on which this walk begins lies some 500m (550 yards) behind the El Palmeral Shopping Centre. You can walk to the beginning of the track by taking the road immediately next to the Hodge Podge clothing shop. This is a one-way system, so if you want to drive you will have to go around the petrol station to the left of the shopping centre, turn right, then take the second left into Calle Playa de la Jacquete. Park at the very end by the pylon where the road ends and the track begins. Almost immediately

Wind generates a growing proportion of the island's electricity

to your left as you begin the walk is the Parque Eólico Cañada de la Barca wind farm. Very little grain is grown in the south of Fuerteventura so conventional windmills are a rare sight, but wind turbines are now beginning to appear on the island and this row of giants, which generates electricity for around 15 per cent of the whole island, makes a convenient landmark.

Wind

Don't do this walk if it is a windy day as you risk being sandblasted and half-blinded by dust and sand.

Swimming

Do take along your swimming kit or simply bare all as many people do on these beaches. There are a few small protected lagoon areas along this stretch where you may (just) be able to immerse yourself completely, but you MUST beware that it is highly dangerous to swim anywhere in open water on the west coast due to the treacherous currents and undertows.

3–4

You reach the west coast after about 40 minutes of walking, emerging at the beach of Agua Tres Piedras. Step down carefully to the beach and look at the weird eroded shapes that have been caused in the alternating layers of basalt and fossilized sand. It may not be apparent to the human eye, but at the base of this escarpment

Los Boquetes **4**

Agua Liques

Agua Tres Piedras **3**

Cañada del Rio

Istmo de la Pared

2 Parque Eólico Cañada de la Barca

0   1 km
0   ½ mile

Centro Commercial El Palmeral **1**

COSTA CALMA

(FV2)

2–3

Many parallel tracks cross the island at this point but simply follow your nose as they all head due west. This is a popular walk so you will rarely be on your own. Away to your right (the northwest) the hills and low mountains often sit broodily. It may be bright sunshine on the trail yet quite dark in the distance.

What you are walking on is a mix of ancient jable (dune field) of solidified sand, covered in saltpetre, and a more recent jable made up of dunes blown across the isthmus by the trade winds from the west coast. The sands are held together by small scrubby plants chewed by goats.

there are natural springs that provide a welcome watering hole for birds and livestock. Continue on to the next large beach area, where a "totem pole" has been made from driftwood and the eroded shapes become more spectacular. A huge sand dune slopes right down to the beach. A little further north black lava outflows provide a lagoon area and rock pools for paddling. The

Taking a break

Take plenty of water with you. The Fuerte Action Bar in the El Palmeral Shopping Centre is a good place for lunch or a snack at the end of your walk.

Ground squirrels and bustards

Ornithologists should keep an eye out for the endangered Canarian *hubara*, a type of bustard endemic to the Canary Islands, which makes its home in La Pared isthmus. Sadly, due to the loss of its habitat, the breeding population in the whole archipelago is down to less than 400 pairs. One creature you are likely to see is the ground squirrel, scampering around the rocks by the seaside.

power of the sea is demonstrated by the large waves which create a spectacular show by breaking off the rocks high into the air. It's an ideal place for older children (► note on Swimming, page 151) but if you're exploring the rock pools beware that some of the crabs around here are quite large!

It takes around another five to ten minutes to walk along the coast to reach Los Boquetes, a spectacular little bay with bright red layers of rock. On the far side, walk out to the end of the point and enjoy great views up and down the coast. A wall of rock blocks progress much further up the coast so it's time to turn back.

4–1

From here you can either return the way you came, which is the easiest option, or negotiate your way over the dunes and return to Costa Calma by paths that run parallel to the one you came on. Break the journey back with a picnic at one of the beaches.

The west coast has enticing beaches, but beware the treacherous currents

Practicalities

Websites
• www.fuerteventuraturismo.com is the official site.
• www.fuerteventura.com is a very good site.
Other sites worth a look are www.fuertenews.com, an English-language weekly magazine and their offshoot island guide, www.fuerteventuragrapevine.net

In the UK
Spanish Tourist Office
2nd floor, 79 New
Cavendish Street,
London W1W 6XB
☎ 020 7486 8077

BEFORE YOU GO

WHAT YOU NEED

		UK	Germany	USA	Canada	Australia	Ireland	Netherlands	Spain
●	Required								
○	Suggested								
▲	Not required								
△	Not applicable								
Passport/National Identity Card		●	●	●	●	●	●	●	●
Visa		▲	▲	▲	▲	▲	▲	▲	▲
Onward or Return Ticket		○	○	▲	▲	▲	▲	○	○
Health Inoculations (tetanus and polio)		▲	▲	▲	▲	▲	▲	▲	▲
Health Documentation (► 158)		●	●	▲	▲	▲	●	●	●
Travel Insurance		○	○	○	○	○	○	○	○
Driver's Licence (national)		●	●	●	●	●	●	●	●
Car Insurance Certificate		●	●	●	●	●	●	●	●
Car Registration Document		●	●	●	●	●	●	●	○

WHEN TO GO

Fuerteventura

(⎯⎯⎯) High season   (⎯⎯⎯) Low season

JAN	FEB	MAR	APR	MAY	JUN	JUL	AUG	SEP	OCT	NOV	DEC
22°C	23°C	26°C	22°C	25°C	26°C	26°C	28°C	26°C	26°C	24°C	23°C
72°F	73°F	79°F	72°F	77°F	79°F	79°F	82°F	79°F	79°F	75°F	73°F

☀ Sun   ☁ Cloud   🌧 Wet   ⛅ Sun/Showers

The temperatures above are the **average daily maximum** for each month. Minimum temperatures rarely drop below 15°C (59°F); a year-round spring climate means that average temperatures range from 19°C (66°F) in winter to 26°C (79°F) in summer. The sea temperature varies from 19°C (66°F) in January to 24°C (75°F) in September. Most of the rain falls in the north and there is occasional snow in the mountains. The north is also affected by the *mar de nubes* ("sea of clouds"), low-lying clouds brought by the trade winds, and the *panza de burro* ("donkey's belly"), a grey haze that produces intense heat in summer. There is a second peak in July and August, when many Spanish families are on holiday. The quietest months are May, June, September and October.

GETTING THERE

By Air

There are numerous charter flights throughout the year from London and other European cities. Most seats are sold by tour operators as part of a package holiday, but it is possible to buy a flight-only deal though travel agents on the internet. For independent travellers, the disadvantage of charter flights is that you are usually restricted to a period of either seven or 14 days.

The Spanish national airline, **Iberia**, operates regular scheduled flights to Fuerteventura, but these are expensive and unless you are already living in Spain they are not worth considering.

If you can get a cheap flight to Lanzarote, but not Fuerteventura, do so then take a ferry (► below) to Corralejo from Puerto del Carmen or Playa Blanca.

Inter-island Travel

By air Binter Canarias (www.binternet.com) offer daily flights from Fuerteventura to the other Canary Islands.
By sea Naviera Armas (tel: 902 456 500, www.naviera-armas.com) operate from Puerto del Rosario to Las Palmas on Gran Canaria and from Morro Bable or Corralejo to Arrecife on Lanzarote. Naviera Armas also operates a service from Morro Jable to Santa Cruz de Tenerife on the island of Tenerife.

There is also a regular ferry service between Fuerteventura and Lanzarote from Corralejo to Playa Blanca and from Correlajo to Puerto del Carmen.

TIME

Unlike the rest of Spain, the Canary Islands observe Greenwich Mean Time (GMT). Summer time (GMT+1) operates from the last Sunday in March to the last Sunday in October.

CURRENCY AND FOREIGN EXCHANGE

Currency As in the rest of Spain, the Canary Islands have adopted the euro. Notes are in denominations of 5, 10, 20, 50, 100, 200, 500; coins come in 1, 2, 5, 10, 20 and 50 cents and 1 and 2 euros.
Credit Cards Major credit cards are widely accepted in the resorts, but don't rely on these elsewhere.
Exchange Banks generally offer the best rates for changing foreign currency and travellers' cheques though money can be exchanged at travel agents, hotels and exchange bureaux. When changing travellers' cheques you will need to show your passport. You can also withdraw cash from **ATM (cashpoint) machines** using your credit or debit card and PIN. The rate of exchange is often better than what you will get elsewhere though your account holder will usually make a charge for this service.

Practicalities 155

GMT
12 noon

Fuerteventura
noon

→

mainland Spain
1pm

→

Germany
1pm

←

USA (NY)
7am

WHEN YOU ARE THERE

CLOTHING SIZES

UK	Rest of Europe	USA	
36	46	36	Suits
38	48	38	
40	50	40	
42	52	42	
44	54	44	
46	56	46	
7	41	8	Shoes
7.5	42	8.5	
8.5	43	9.5	
9.5	44	10.5	
10.5	45	11.5	
11	46	12	
14.5	37	14.5	Shirts
15	38	15	
15.5	39/40	15.5	
16	41	16	
16.5	42	16.5	
17	43	17	
8	34	6	Dresses
10	36	8	
12	38	10	
14	40	12	
16	42	14	
18	44	16	
4.5	38	6	Shoes
5	38	6.5	
5.5	39	7	
6	39	7.5	
6.5	40	8	
7	41	8.5	

NATIONAL HOLIDAYS

1 Jan	New Year's Day
6 Jan	Epiphany
2 Feb	Candlemas
19 Mar	St Joseph's Day
Mar/Apr	Good Friday, Easter Monday
1 May	Labour Day
30 May	Canary Islands' Day
May/June	Corpus Christi
25 July	St James
15 Aug	Assumption of the Virgin
12 Oct	Columbus Day
1 Nov	All Saints' Day
6 Dec	Constitution Day
8 Dec	Feast of the Immaculate Conception
25 Dec	Christmas Day

OPENING HOURS

○ Shops   ● Post Offices
● Offices   ○ Museums
● Banks   ○ Pharmacies

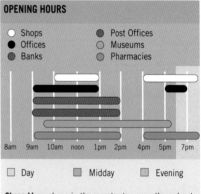

8am 9am 10am noon 1pm 2pm 4pm 5pm 7pm

□ Day   ▨ Midday   ▨ Evening

Shops Many shops in the resorts stay open throughout the day. Most shops are closed on Sundays.
Banks Banks are closed on Sundays.
Restaurants Many restaurants in the larger resorts are open daily from around 10am to midnight.
Museums and attractions Most museums are open Tuesday to Friday and Sunday 9:30am–5:30pm.

POLICE/FIRE/AMBULANCE 112

PERSONAL SAFETY

Crime is not a problem in Fuerteventura. The greatest risk of theft is from another tourist. Put all belongings out of sight in the boot of your car when you are parked. If you are in self-catering accommodation lock all windows and doors before going out.

In an emergency call the police on 112 from any phone.

Police assistance:
☎ **112** from any phone

ELECTRICITY

The power supply is 220 volts. Sockets take continental-style two-pin plugs. Visitors from the UK will require an adaptor, available at the airport and in the resorts.

TELEPHONES

The cheapest way of making calls is to go to a *locutorio*. These can be found all over the island, in shopping centres or even as part of a local grocer's or souvenir shop. You are allocated a booth and then charged for the call afterwards. They are very cheap indeed and a 20-minute call to mainland Europe in the evening costs little more than a couple of euros.

There are public telephones on most street corners with instructions in several languages. Most take coins or phonecards (*tarjetas telefónicas*), which are available from several outlets, though in practice they are not always stocked. The cheap rate for international calls applies 10pm to 8am and all day Sunday.

International Dialling Codes
Dial 00 followed by
UK:	44
Ireland:	353
Germany:	49
USA:	1

POST

Post boxes are yellow and often have a slot marked *extranjeros* for mail abroad. Stamps (*sellos*) are available from post offices, hotels, news kiosks, tobacconists and some postcard shops.

A postcard to the UK or northern Europe will usually take about 7–10 days.

TIPS/GRATUITIES

Tipping is not expected for all services, and rates are lower than in some countries. As a general guide:

Restaurants	5–10%
Cafés/bars	Discretion
Tour guides	Discretion
Taxis	10%
Hairdressers	10%
Hotel staff	10%
Lavatories	Discretion

CONSULATES and EMBASSIES

UK ☎ 928 262 508	**Ireland** ☎ 928 297 725	**Germany** ☎ 928 491 880	**Switzerland** ☎ 928 261 751	**Austria** ☎ 928 762 500

HEALTH

 Insurance Citizens of the European Union and certain other countries receive free medical treatment in Spain with the relevant documentation, although private medical insurance is still advised and is essential for all other visitors.

 Dental Services Dental treatment has to be paid for by all visitors but is usually covered by private medical insurance.

 Weather Visitors from cooler countries are especially vulnerable to the effects of the sun. You should cover up with a high-factor sunblock and drink plenty of non-alcoholic fluids. Children need to be well protected, especially when playing near the sea, as water and sand reflect the sun's rays.

 Drugs Prescription and non-prescription drugs and medicines are available from pharmacies, usually distinguished by a large green cross. Outside normal hours, a notice on the door of each pharmacy should give the address of the nearest duty pharmacist.

 Safe Water Tap water is generally safe to drink but has a high salt content. Mineral water is widely available and cheap, especially when bought at supermarkets in 5-litre (1.3-gallon) containers.

CONCESSIONS

Students In general the Canary Islands do not attract backpacking youngsters and there are few if any youth or student concessions. There are no youth hostels or campsites on the island although there is a basic campsite on Isla de Lobos.

Senior Citizens Fuerteventura is an excellent destination for older travellers, especially in winter when the climate is clement. Some hotels and apartments offer long-stay discounts. The best deals are available through tour operators who specialise in holidays for senior citizens.

TRAVELLING WITH A DISABILITY

All new buildings in Spain have to be equipped with wheelchair access, but many older hotels, apartment blocks and public buildings are still inaccessible. Some buses have doors that lower to ground level for wheelchair access. Before booking a holiday, you should discuss your particular needs with your tour operator or hotel.

CHILDREN

Hotels and restaurants are generally very child-friendly, and many hotels have playgrounds, parks, mini-golf and children's pools. Some tour operators also provide children's clubs and activities as part of your holiday. However, facilities such as baby-changing rooms are rare.

LAVATORIES

There are public lavatories in shopping centres and at some larger beaches. Other useful standbys are museums and bars.

CUSTOMS

The import of wildlife souvenirs sourced from rare or endangered species may be either illegal or require a special permit. Before buying, check your home country's customs regulations.

Useful Words and Phrases

Yes/no **Sí/no**
Please **Por favor**
Thank you **Gracias**
You're welcome **De nada**
Hello **Hola**
Goodbye **Adiós**
Good morning **Buenos días**
Good afternoon **Buenas tardes**
Good night **Buenas noches**
How are you? **¿Qué tal?**
How much is this? **¿Cuánto vale?**
I'm sorry **Lo siento**
Excuse me **Perdone**
I'd like… **Me gustaría…**
Open **Abierto**
Closed **Cerrado**

Today **Hoy**
Tomorrow **Mañana**
Yesterday **Ayer**
Monday **Lunes**
Tuesday **Martes**
Wednesday **Miércoles**
Thursday **Jueves**
Friday **Viernes**
Saturday **Sábado**
Sunday **Domingo**

DIRECTIONS

I'm lost **Me he perdido**
Where is…? **¿Dónde está…?**
How do I get to…?
 ¿Cómo se va…?
 the bank **al banco**

the post office
 a la oficina de correos
Where are the lavatories?
 ¿Dónde están los servicios?
Left **a la izquierda**
Right **a la derecha**
Straight on **todo recto**
At the traffic lights **en el semáforo**

IF YOU NEED HELP

Help! **¡Socorro! / ¡Ayuda!**
Could you help me, please
 ¿Podría ayudarme, por favor?
Do you speak English? **¿Habla inglés?**
I don't understand **No entiendo**
I don't speak Spanish
 No hablo español
Could you call a doctor?
 **¿Podría llamar a un médico,
 por favor?**

ACCOMMODATION

Do you have a single/double room?
 **¿Le queda alguna habitación
 individual/doble?**
 with/without bath/WC/shower
 **con/sin baño propio/
 lavabo propio/ducha propia**
Does that include breakfast?
 ¿Incluye desayuno?
I'll take this room
 Me quedo con esta habitación
The key to room…, please
 **La llave de la habitación…,
 por favor**

NUMBERS

1	uno	11	once	21	veintiuno	200	doscientos
2	dos	12	doce	22	veintidós	300	trescientos
3	tres	13	trece	30	treinta	400	cuatrocientos
4	cuatro	14	catorce	40	cuarenta	500	quinientos
5	cinco	15	quince	50	cincuenta	600	seiscientos
6	seis	16	dieciséis	60	sesenta	700	setecientos
7	siete	17	diecisiete	70	setenta	800	ochocientos
8	ocho	18	dieciocho	80	ochenta	900	novecientos
9	nueve	19	diecinueve	90	noventa	1000	mil
10	diez	20	veinte	100	cien		

I'd like to book a table
Me gustaría reservar una mesa
Have you got a table for two, please?
¿Tienen una mesa para dos
personas, por favor?
Could we see the menu, please?
¿Nos podría traer la carta, por favor?
Could I have the bill, please?
¿La cuenta, por favor?
service charge included
servicio incluido

breakfast **el desayuno**
lunch **el almuerzo**
dinner **la cena**
table **una mesa**
waiter/waitress **camarero/camarera**
starters **las entradas**
main course **los platos principales**
desserts **postres**
dish of the day **plato del día**
bill **la cuenta**

MENU READER

aceituna olive
ajo garlic
alcachofa
artichoke
almejas clams
almendras
almonds
anguila eel
arroz rice
atún/bonito tuna

bacalao cod
berenjena
aubergine
(eggplant)
biftec steak
bocadillo sandwich
boquerones
anchovies

calamares squid
caldo broth
callos tripe
cangrejo crab
cebolla onion
cerdo pork
cerezas cherries
cerveza beer
champiñones
mushrooms
chorizo spicy
sausage
chuleta chop
churros fritters
ciruela plum
cochinillo asado
roast suckling pig
codorniz quail
conejo rabbit
cordero lamb

crema cream
criadillas
sweetbreads
crudo raw

endibia chicory
ensalada (mixta)
mixed salad
ensaladilla rusa
Russian salad
espárragos
asparagus
espinaca spinach

fideos noodles
filete fillet
flan crème caramel
frambuesa
raspberry
fresa strawberry
fruta (de
temporade)
seasonal fruit

galleta biscuit
(cookie)
gambas prawns
garbanzos
chickpeas
gazpacho andaluz
gazpacho (cold
soup)
grosellas red/black
currants
guisantes peas

habas broad beans
helado ice cream
hígado de oca
goose liver

huevos fritos/
revueltos
fried/scrambled
eggs

jamón ham
judías verdes
French beans
jugo fruit juice

langosta lobster
langostino
crayfish
leche milk
lechuga lettuce
legumbres
vegetables
lengua tongue
lenguado sole
liebre hare
lomo de cerdo
pork tenderloin

manzana apple
mariscos seafood
mejillones
mussels
melocotón peach
melón melon
merluza hake
mero sea bass
morcilla black
pudding

pan bread
panceta streaky
bacon
pato duck
pepinillos
gherkins

pepino cucumber
pera pear
perdiz partridge
perejil parsley
pescado fish
pez espada
swordfish
pimientos red/
green peppers
piña pineapple
plátano banana
pollo chicken
puerro leek
pulpo octopus

queso cheese

rape monkfish
riñones kidneys
rodaballo turbot

salchicha sausage
salchichón salami
salmón salmon
salmonete red
mullet
solomillo sirloin
sopa soup

tortilla española
Spanish
omelette
tortilla francesa
plain omelette
trucha trout

verduras green
vegetables

zanahorias carrots

Atlas

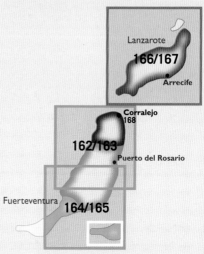

Lanzarote

166/167

Arrecife

Corralejo
168

162/163

Puerto del Rosario

Fuerteventura **164/165**

Las Palmas
169

Gran Canaria

To identify the regions, see the map on the inside of the front cover

Regional Maps

▬▬▬ Major route		☐	Main town
▬▬▬ Motorway		▫	Town
▬▬▬ Main road		○	Village
▬▬ Other road		○	Small village
⋯⋯ Track		▣	Featured place of interest
National/regional park		▪	Place of interest
Built-up area		✈	Airport

162-165 0 1 2 3 4 5 km / 0 1 2 3 miles

166/167 0 1 2 3 4 5 km / 0 1 2 3 miles

Streetplan

▬▬ Motorway			Park
▬▬ Main road		■	Important building
▬▬ Other road		▣	Featured place of interest
▬▬ Ferry		i	Information

168 0 50 100 150 200 250 metres / 0 50 100 150 200 250 yards

169 0 250 500 750 metres / 0 250 500 750 yards

A B C

5

4

3

2

1

Punta Blanca

Punta de Tostón
o de la Ballena

Caleta del Rio

Playa de Marfolin

El Cotillo — El Roque
FV10

Playa del Castillo

Playa del Aljibe de la Cueva

Playa del Águila

Punta de Taca

Playa de Esquinzo

309m
Montaña
de la Blanca

Laderas de la Manta

Barranco de Esquinzo

Punta de Paso Chico

Playa de Tebeto

Tindaya

Playa de la Mujer

Playa de Jarubio

Monumento a Don
Miguel de Unamuno

El Malpaís Delgado
366m
Montaña
Quemada

251m
Montaña
Blanca

Barranco de Molinos

Los Molinos

FV207

FV221
Tefia

Ecomuseo de
La Alcogida

Tefia de
Arriba

326m
Atalaya de
Risco Grande

316m
Montaña
Bermeja

*Embalse de
los Molinos*

FV207
417m
Montaña
de Tao

Playa de los Mozos
Playa de Santa Inés
Playa del Valle

Bco. de los Mozos

Llanos de la
Concepción

FV30

542m
Montaña
del Campo

Residencial
Aguas Verdes

Casas de
Almácigo

La Ampuyenta

Punta de los Caletones

Valle de
Santa Inés

Barranco de Janey

164

666m
Morro de la
Fuente Vieja

Mirador
de Morro
Veloso

FV416

165
FV20

Punta de la Herradura

Maninubre

Centro de
Artesanía
Molino

Punta del Tarajalito

419m
Montaña
Aceituno

Convento de
San Buenaventura

FV413

Betancuria

Antigua

Caleta Negra

670m
Morro Tabaiba

724m
Montaña
Atalaya

FV30

674m
Morro Janana

Bco. de Madre del Agua

Ajuy
FV621

Vega de
Rio Palmas

Valles de
Ortega

FV50

Playa de los Muertos

Ermita de Virgen
de la Peña

Iglesia de
Nuestra
Señora
de la Peña

708m
Gran
Montaña

Agua de
Bueyes

FV415

FV30

Casillas
de Morales

Playa de la Solapa

FV20

416m
Mézquez

Iglesia Nuestra
Señora de Regal

Centro de
Interpretación
de los Molinos

463m
Montaña
Gairia

*Playa de
Garcey*

273m
Montaña

Toto

Pájara

Tiscamanita
Cruz de Piedra

American Star

Playa Blanca (Lanzarote)
Puerto del Carmen (Lanzarote)

Punta Martiño

Parque Natural
del Islote
de Lobos
127m
Montaña
de la Caldera
Isla de Lobos

Playa de la Arena

El Puertito

Punta
Lala
Punta Gorda

Punta de
los Lavaderos

Corralejo

Majanicho

Playa de
la Calera
Punta de Tivas
Flag Beach

Sendero de
Bayuyo
271m
Volcan de
Bayuyo

Puerto
Remedio

162m
Calderón
Hondo

FV101

Playa Bajo Negro

Playa de los Matos

Parque
Natural
de las Dunas
de Corralejo

Playa del Moro

Playa Alzada

Lajares

FV109

Playita del Poris

232m
Montaña
de la Lengua

La Rosita

FV101

FV1

Playa de la Cabezuela

FV10

421m
Montaña
de Arena

Villaverde

353m

314m
Montaña
Roja

533m
Montaña
de Caima

Montaña de
Ecanfraga

Playa de los Picachos

La Oliva

387m
Montaña
de Frontón

FV10

Parque
Holandés

Casas del
Jablito

Montaña
Tindaya

509m
Morro
Carnero

Caldereta

Valle de Fimapaire

Punta del
Tarajalito

Vallebrón

Barranco de Vallebrón

Barranco de Tinojay

Casas de las
Llanadas

689m
Montaña
de la Muda

Guisguey

Playa de los Valdivias

La Matilla

El Time

FV214

FV1

Cabo del Agua

Playito del Charquito

688m
Cerro de
Aceituna

FV10

511m
Cerro de
Temejereque

Puerto Lajas

Tetir

Los Enstancos

FV10

Bco de Monja

595m
Pico de la
Fortaleza

La Asomada

FV3

Urbanización
Rosa de la Monja

439m

FV225

FV10

Majada Marcial

Arrecife (Lanzarote)

P I Risco Prieto

PUERTO
DEL ROSARIO

FV20

Tesjuates

FV20 276m

FV3

Casillas
del Ángel

Llano
Pelado

Montaña de
las Veredas

Los
Pozos

Llano del
Sol

Las Palmas
(Gran Canaria)

FV413

Barranco de Río Cabras

FV2

596m
Rosa del
Taro

483m
Morro
Pinacho

165

El Matorral

Triquivijate

Barranco de Jenejey

Barranco de la Muley

Nuevo
Horizonte

417m
Buenavista

193m
Montaña Blanca
de Abajo

Caleta de
Fuste

FV2

Casas de
Majada Blanca

Casas de
El Cortijo

Salinas del
Carmen

FV50

Playa del Muellito

FV2

497m

Puerto de la Torre

433m

Barranco de Monte Agudo

D   E   F

A B C

Barranco de Janey

Punta de la Herradura

Punta del Tarajalito

666m
Morro de la
Fuente Vieja

419m
Montaña
Aceituno

724m
Montaña
Atalaya

670m
Morro Tabaiba

Caleta Negra

Ajuy

Bco de Madre del Agua

FV621

Vega de
Río Palmas

Playa de los Muertos

Ermita de Virgen
de la Peña

Iglesia de
Nuestra
Señora
de la Peña

Playa de la Solapa

FV30

Playa de
Garcey

American Star

162

416m
Mézque

273m
Montaña
Blanca

Iglesia Nuestra
Señora de Regal

Toto

Pájara

Punta Peñón Blanco

FV605

370m
Lomo de
las Perlas

608m
Carbón

Bco de Vigocho

334m
Montaña
Entresalar

Punta del Gavioto

385m
Montaña
Gavioto

360m
Morro del
Tababejo

Fayagua

481m
Montaña
Pasos

FV511

Playa Amanay
Punta Amanay

Barranco Amanay

528m
Sisacumbre

Tesejerague

Playa de Terife

FV605

FV618

Cardon

345m
Montaña
Tirba

694m
Cardón

Chilegua

Cardón

Playa Negras

Playa de Ugán

FV617

Las Hermosas

FV2

Barranco de los Canales

467m
Caracol

FV529

Punta de Guadelupe

La Pared

313m
Morro de los
Gatos

Playa de la Pared

FV56

Giniginámar

Urbanización
Panorama

Bco de Tarajal

La Lajita
Oasis Park

FV2

Tarajalejo

Punta del
Morrete

FV605

La Lajita

Punta del
Caracol

Agua Tres
Piedras

Jardín Botánico

Playa de
Tarajalejo

Cañada del Río

FV2

Istmo
de la Pared

Playa de
la Lajita

Playas Matas Blancas

Playa de
Barlovento

Costa Calma

Playa Barca

Jandía

de

322m
Loma Negra

Esmeralda
Jandía

Playa de Sotavento

Peninsula

Playas de Jandía

FV2

Casas de
Risco del Paso

Risco del
Paso

Urbanización
Esquinzo
Marabu

Monte
del Mar

Playa de Butihondo

Jandía Playa

A B C

5

4

3

2

1

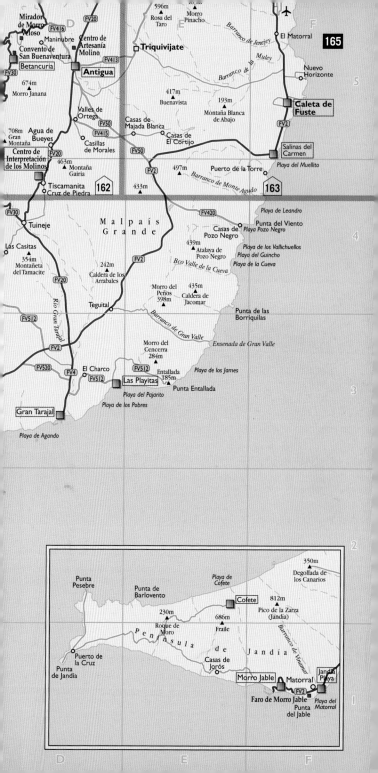

Lanzarote

La Isleta

La Santa

LZ20

Piedra
Mansa

Tenesar

El
Cuchillo

Tinajo

LZ20

Mancha
Blanca

LZ46

312m

Punta de
la Ensenada

Centro de Visitantes e
Interpretación
de Mancha Blanca

LZ67

LZ56

459m

LZ58

Mar de Lava

PARQUE NACIONAL DE TIMANFAYA

Montañas del
Fuego de Timanfaya 511m

507m

LZ30

Echadero de
los Camellos

El Golfo

Charco de
los Clicos

LZ67

La Geria

LZ702

LZ704

La Geria

603m

La Asomada

Los Hervideros

LZ30

Mácher

La Hoya

Uga

LZ30

Yaiza

Salinas de
Janubio

Las Breñas

609m

LZ702

Femés

Las Casitas

LZ2

Mácher
Bajo

La Tiñosa

LZ505

Puerto Calero

Puerto del
Carmen

Punta
de Piedra Alta

Playa Quemada

Bahía de Ávila

Punta Gorda

LZ701

El Rubicón

LZ2

561m

Los Ajaches

La Punta
del Carajao

Punta Ginés

Corralejo (Fuerteventura)

145m

Montaña Roja

Montaña Roja

Playa
Blanca

Las Coloradas

Punta
Pechiguera

Corralejo (Fuerteventura)

Punta del Papagayo

Isla de
Montaña Clara

El Río de
Montaña Clara

Punta Gorda

Playa de las
Conchas

Isla la Graciosa

Punta del Bajío

266m
Montaña
Pedro Barba

Pedro Barba

Punta Fariones

Caleta del Sebo

Orzola

El Río

Mirador
del Río

Punta Prieta

Playa
de la
Cocina

Ye

LZ203

Malpaís de la Corona

605m
Monte
Coronat

Guinate

LZ201

Cueva de
los Verdes

LZ1

Máguez

Haría

Jameos del Agua

LZ10

Punta Mujeres

Punta
de Penedo

Bahía de
Penedo

El Risco de Famara

LZ206

Tabayesco

Arrieta

La Caleta
de Famara

672m
Peñas
del Chache

Caleta de
Caballo

LZ401

Mala Abajo
Punta Pasito

Mala

El Jable

Las Laderas

Sóo

Los Valles

Charco del Palo

LZ405

Jardín de Cactus

Muñique

LZ402

Guatiza

LZ10

Teseguite

Tiagua

Teguise

LZ1

La Vegueta

LZ30

Castillo de
Santa Bárbara

Playa del Tío Joaquín

Tao

Nazaret

Ensenada de
los Barranquillos

LZ408

229m
Cerro Hurón

Casa Museo y
El Monumento
al Campesino

Tahiche

El Grifo

LZ30

LZ34

Costa Teguise

LZ34

San
Bartolomé

Fundación
César Manrique

LZ1

Montaña
Blanca

LZ20

Argana Baja

Castillo de
San José

Playa Honda

LZ2

ARRECIFE

Tías

Playa de
Matagorda

Castillo de
San Gabriel

LZ506

Las Costas

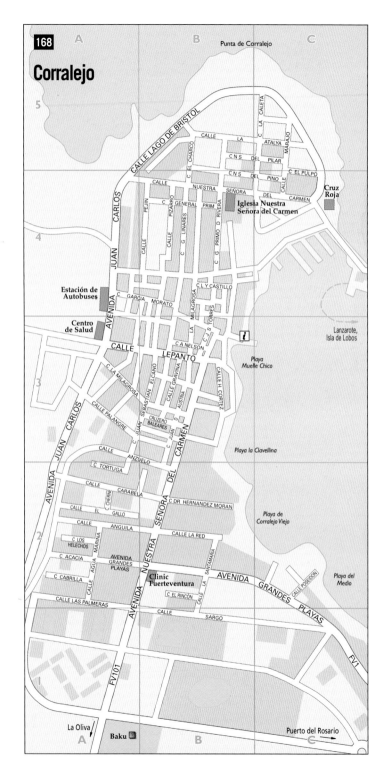

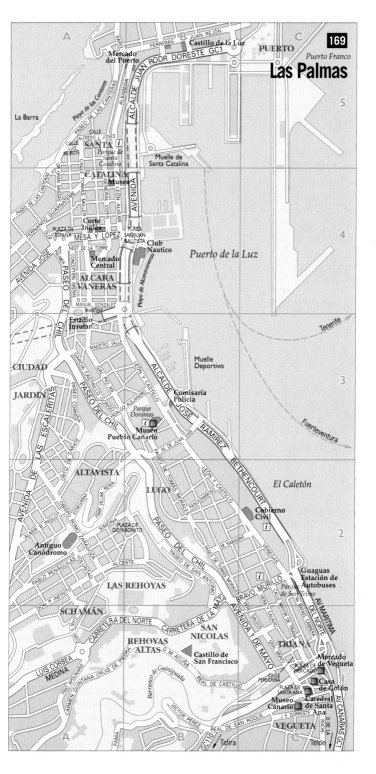

Islas Canarias

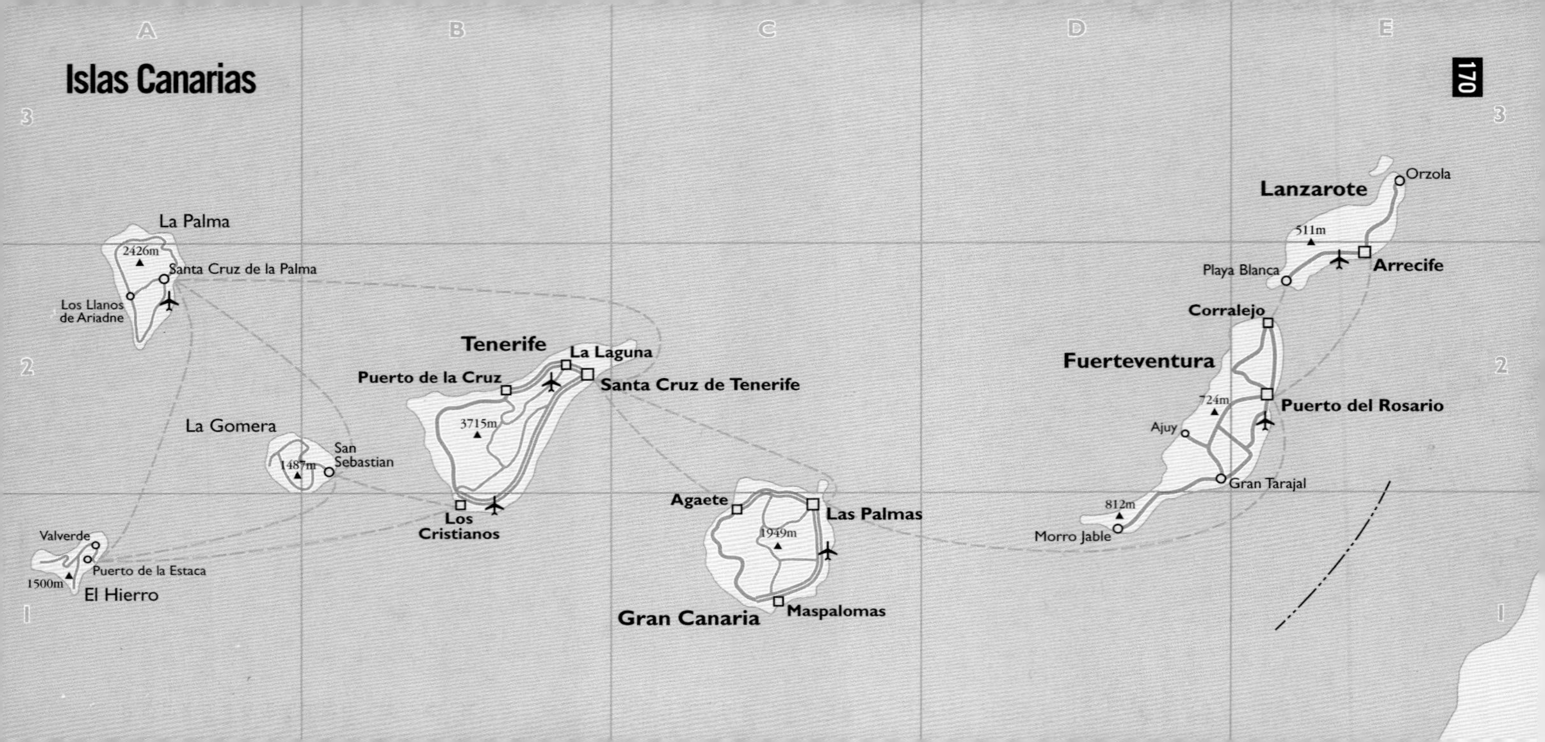

La Palma

2426m ▲

Santa Cruz de la Palma

Los Llanos
de Ariadne

La Gomera

San
Sebastian

1487m ▲

Valverde

1500m ▲

Puerto de la Estaca

El Hierro

Tenerife

Puerto de la Cruz

La Laguna

Santa Cruz de Tenerife

3715m ▲

Los
Cristianos

Agaete

Las Palmas

1949m ▲

Gran Canaria

Maspalomas

Lanzarote

Orzola

Arrecife

511m ▲

Playa Blanca

Corralejo

Puerto del Rosario

Fuerteventura

724m ▲

Ajuy

Gran Tarajal

812m ▲

Morro Jable

Index

accommodation 38–39
  central Fuerteventura 82
  the North 61–62
  the South 103–104
  useful words and phrases
    159
admission charges 38
Agua Tres Piedras 151
airports and air services
  Fuerteventura 36, 155
  Gran Canaria 128
Ajuy 77
  Caleta Negra 66, 77
Animal Experience 49
Antigua 73, 149
  Centro de Artesanía
    Molino 73, 149
  Nuestra Señora de
    Antigua 73
apartments 39
aquarium 76, 84
Arrecife 110, 122–123
  Castillo de San Gabriel
    122
  Castillo de San José 123
  Iglesia de San Ginés 123
  Museo Internacional de
    Arte Contemporáneo
    123
Atlantis Myth 30
ATM (cashpoint) machines
  155
Ayoze 10

Baku 22, 49
banks 155, 156
Barley Beach 97
Barlovento 86, 91
barrancos 6
bars 42
beaches 23, 32
Betancuria 23, 66, 70–72,
  148
  Casa Santa María 71, 72
  Convento de San
    Buenaventura 71
  Iglesia de Santa María
    70–71, 72
  Museo Arqueológico y
    Etnográfico 11, 72
  Museo de Arte Sacro 71,
    72
  Museo Artesanía 34, 71,
    83
Béthencourt, Jean de 9,
  10–11, 51, 70
birdlife 139
boat trips 26, 27, 52, 64,
  84, 106
bodyboarding 22, 64
bowling 22
Burial of the Sardine 16
buses
  Fuerteventura 37
  Gran Canaria 129
cactus gardens

Fuerteventura 73, 94
  Lanzarote 110, 122
Café El Naufragio 29, 75
Caleta de Fuste 66, 76
Caleta Negra 66, 77
camels 8, 25, 94
  camel rides 57, 94, 114,
    115
camping 158
Canary Islands 6, 7
car hire
  Fuerteventura 36, 37–38
  Lanzarote 109
Carnaval 15–16
Casa del Capellán 54
Casa de Colón 132
Casa de los Coroneles 53
Casa Cuartel 118
Casa Mané 54
Casa Museo Unamuno 75
Casa Santa María 71, 72
Casa-Museo Dr Mena 149
casas rurales 8, 39
Casillas del Angel 149
Castillo de San Gabriel 122
Castillo de San José 123
Castillo de Santa Barbara
  119
catamaran trips 52, 64, 84,
  106, 108
Catedral de Santa Ana 134
caves
  Caleta Negra 66, 77
  Cueva Pintada 133
  Cueva de los Verdes 117,
    122
  Cueva Villaverde 56
  Jameos del Agua
    116–117
  Los Hervideros 123
central Fuerteventura
  65–84
  accommodation 82
  Ajuy 77
  Antigua 73, 149
  Betancuria 23, 66, 70–72
  Caleta de Fuste 66, 76
  Centro de Interpretación
    de los Molinos 78
  eating out 79–81
  Ecomuseo de La
    Alcogida 8, 33, 66, 74,
    146
  entertainment 84
  Gran Tarajal 78
  Las Playitas 78
  Los Molinos 75
  map 66–7
  Pájara 78
  Puerto del Rosario 66,
    75
  Salinas del Carmen 66,
    76
  shopping 83
  two-day itinerary 68–69
  Vega de Río Palmas 77,
    148
Centro de Arte Canario
  (CAC) 53–54

Centro de Artesanía
  Molino 73, 149
Centro de Interpretación
  de los Molinos 78
Charco de los Clicos 120
children 158
  eating out 40
  entertainment 22–23, 97
climate and seasons 154
clothing sizes 156
clubs 42
cochineal 121
Cofete 92, 98–99
coffee 21, 41
Columbus, Christopher
  132
concessions 158
consulates and embassies
  158
Convento de San
  Buenaventura 71
Convento de San Francisco
  118
Convento de Santo
  Domingo 118, 119
Corralejo 8, 44, 48–50,
  145
  Baku 22, 49
  Flag Beach 50
  Glass Beach 50
  Parque Natural de las
    Dunas de Corralejo 50
  Playa Galera 49
  Villa Tabaiba Galeria de
    Arte 50
Costa Calma 86, 90, 92,
  96, 150
crafts 41–42, 83
credit cards 155
crime and personal safety
  157
Cueva Pintada 133
Cueva del Llanos 56
Cueva de los Verdes 117,
  122
Cueva Villaverde 56
currency 155
customs regulations 158

Degollada de los
  Granadillos 148
dental services 158
disabilities, travellers with
  158
diving 23, 27, 42, 64, 84,
  106
Dolphin Safari 26
drinking water 40, 158
driving 37–38, 98, 154
  see also walks and drives
drugs and medicines 158

eating out 33, 39–41
  central Fuerteventura
    79–81
  Gran Canaria 135
  Lanzarote 124–125
  mealtimes 40
  menu reader 160

the North 58–60
the South 100–102
tipping 40
useful words and
  phrases 160
Echadero de los Camellos
  114
Ecomuseo de La Alcogida
  8, 33, 66, 74, 146
El Cotillo 8, 23, 44, 55
  Fortaleza/Torre del Tostón
  55
El Golfo 120, 123
El Hotel del Terror 49
El Puertito 51, 52, 138
El Río 121
electricity 157
Embalse de las Peñitas 148
embroidery 55, 63
emergencies 157
  useful words and
  phrases 159
entertainment 42
  central Fuerteventura 84
  the North 64
  the South 106
Ermita de La Virgen de la
  Peña 17, 77
Ermita de San Pedro de
  Alcántara 149
Esquinzo 96

farming 7
Faro de Lobos 140
Faro de Morro Jable 96
ferries
  Fuerteventura 36
  Gran Canaria 128, 155
  Lanzarote 36, 108, 155
festivals and events 15–17,
  23, 42
fishing 26, 64, 106
fishing industry 8
Flag Beach 50
food and drink 18–21,
  39–41
  coffee 21, 41
  drinking water 40, 158
  goats' cheese 19, 83
  specialities 18–21, 42
  tapas 21, 40
  vegetarian food 20–21,
  40
  wines and spirits 21, 41,
  109, 120
  see also eating out
foreign exchange 155
Fortaleza/Torre del Tostón
  55
fuel 38
Fundación César Manrique
  120–121
FV Massira 28

gifts and souvenirs 41–42
Glass Beach 50
glass-bottomed boats 27,
  52, 84
go-karting 84

goats 8, 19, 24–25
goats' cheese 19, 83
golf 42, 84, 106
Gran Canaria 127–136
  eating out 135
  Las Palmas 130–134
  shopping 136
  tourist information 129
  travelling around 129
  travelling to 128–129
Gran Moñtana 149
Gran Tarajal 78
Guanches 9–10, 11, 57,
  133
Guize 10, 53

Hammer, Jo 55, 56
Haría 110, 121
  Museo de Arte Sacro
  121
health 154, 158
history 9–11
hornitos 140
horseriding 84
Hotel Rural Mahoh 56, 60,
  145
hoteles rurales 8, 39
hotels 33, 39
  see also accommodation

Iglesia de Nuestra Señora
  de la Candelaria 53
Iglesia de Nuestra Señora
  de Guadalupe 118
Iglesia Nuestra Señora del
  Rosario 75
Iglesia de San Ginés 123
Iglesia de Santa María
  70–71, 72
insurance 154, 158
inter-island travel 155
  see also ferries
International Kite Festival
  23
International Museum of
  Contemporary Art 123
Isla de Lobos 23, 34, 44,
  51–52
  El Puertito 51, 52, 138
  Faro de Lobos 51, 140
  Las Lagunitas 139
  Montaña de la Caldera
  32, 140–141
  Playa la Concha 23, 141
  walk 138–141
Isla la Graciosa 121

Jameos del Agua 110,
  116–117
Jandía Playa 86, 92, 96–97
  Faro de Morro Jable 96
Jardín Botánico 95
Jardín de Cactus 110, 122
jet skiing 64, 106
jetfoil service 36

kite flying 23
kiteboarding 12, 13, 42,
  64, 106

La Ampuyenta 149
  Casa-Museo Dr Mena
  149
  Ermita de San Pedro de
  Alcántara 149
La Geria 120
La Lajita Oasis Park 22,
  25, 31, 93–95
La Oliva 44, 53–54, 145
  Casa del Capellán 54
  Casa de los Coroneles 53
  Casa Mané 54
  Centro de Arte Canario
  (CAC) 53–54
  Iglesia de Nuestra Señora
  de la Candelaria 53
  Museo del Grano La
  Cilla 54
La Pared 86, 96, 150
La Rosita 56–57
Lajares 44, 55–56
  School of Embroidery
  55, 63
landscape 6
language 159–160
Lanzarote 107–126
  Arrecife 110, 122–123
  Cueva de los Verdes 122
  eating out 124–125
  El Golfo 120, 123
  Fundación César
  Manrique 120–121
  Haría 110, 121
  Jameos del Agua 110,
  116–117
  Jardín de Cactus 110,
  122
  La Geria 120
  map 110–111
  Mirador del Río 110,
  121–122
  one-day itinerary
  112–113
  Parque Nacional de
  Timanfaya 110,
  114–115
  Puerto del Carmen 108,
  110, 123
  shopping 109, 126
  Teguise 110, 118–119
  tourist information 109
  travelling around 109
  travelling to 108
Las Lagunitas 139
Las Palmas 130–134
  Casa de Colón 132
  Catedral de Santa Ana
  134
  map 131
  Mercado de Vegueta 134
  Museo Canario 133
  Museo Elder 134
  Museo Néstor 134
  Museo Pueblo Canario
  134
  Parque de San Telmo
  134
  Parque de Santa Catalina
  134

Playa de las Canteras 130
Puerto de la Luz 130
Vegueta 130
Las Playitas 78
lavatories 158
locusts 8
Los Boquetes 152
Los Hervideros 123
Los Molinos 75

Majanicho 144
majoreros 7, 10, 11
malpaís 6, 44, 142
Manrique, César 73, 108, 109, 114, 116, 120–121, 122, 123
Manrique's House 120–121
Martínez, Tinín 31
markets 42
medical treatment 158
menu reader 160
Mercado de Vegueta 134
Mirador de Morro Veloso 33, 148
Mirador del Río 110, 121–122
miradores 37
money 155
Montaña de la Caldera 32, 140–141
Montaña Colorada 142
Montaña Quemada 146
Montaña Tindaya 11, 30, 44, 57
Montaña Tindaya Cube 30, 34
Montañas del Fuego 114–115
Morro Jable 86, 97–98
motorbike tours 84
mountain biking 84
Museo Arqueológico y Etnográfico 11, 72
Museo de Arte Sacro (Betancuria) 71, 72
Museo de Arte Sacro (Haría) 121
Museo Artesanía 34, 71, 83
Museo Canario 133
Museo Elder 134
Museo del Grano La Cilla 54
Museo Internacional de Arte Contemporáneo 123
Museo Néstor 134
Museo Pueblo Canario 134
Museo de Sal 76
museum opening hours 156

national holidays 156
National Protected Spaces 31
nightlife 42
the North 43–64
accommodation 61–62
Corralejo 8, 44, 48–50

eating out 58–60
El Cotillo 8, 23, 44, 55
entertainment 64
four-day itinerary 46–47
Isla de Lobos 23, 34, 44, 51–52
La Oliva 44, 53–54, 145
Lajares 44, 55–56
map 44–45
Montaña Tindaya 11, 44, 57
shopping 63
Villaverde 44, 56–57, 145
nudist beach 92
Nuestra Señora de Antigua 73
Nuestra Señora de la Regla 78

Oasis Park 22, 25, 31, 93–95
Oceanarium Explorer 26, 84
off-road driving 30, 38, 98
office hours 156
olivine 109, 120
opening hours 41, 156

Pájara 78, 148
Nuestra Señora de la Regla 78
Palacio del Marqués 118, 119
Palacio Spínola 118, 119
parking 38
Parque Eólico Cañada de la Barca 150
Parque Nacional de Timanfaya 110, 114–115
Parque Natural de las Dunas de Corralejo 50
Parque de San Telmo 134
Parque de Santa Catalina 134
passports and visas 154
Pendón de la Conquista 71
pharmacies 156, 158
Pico de la Fraile 98
Pico de la Zarza 98
Playa Barca 90
Playa de Barlovento 92
Playa Blanca 108
Playa de Butihondo 92
Playa de las Canteras 130
Playa de Cebada 97
Playa de la Concha 23, 141
Playa Galera 49
Playa del Matorral 92
Playa de Sotavento 91
Playas de Jandía 90–92
Playas Lagos 55
podomorphs 57
police 157
population 7
postal services 156, 157
public transport 37
Puerto del Carmen 108, 110, 123

Puerto de la Luz 130
Puerto Peña *see* Ajuy
Puerto del Rosario 66, 75
Café El Naufragio 29, 75
Casa Museo Unamuno 75
Iglesia Nuestra Señora del Rosario 75

quad bikes 64, 84

Rejón, Juan 130
religious festivals 17
restaurants *see* eating out
Risco del Paso 34, 91
Romero, Maria Lazaga 31
Rose of Sharon 28
Ruta de los Volcanes 115

Salinas del Carmen 66, 76
Museo de Sal 76
Salinas de Janubio 123
salt flats 76, 123
Salt Museum 76
sand dunes 31, 50
sand sculptures 49
School of Embroidery 55, 63
self-catering accommodation 39
Sendero de Bayuyo 142–144
senior citizens 158
shipwrecks 28–29
shopping 34, 41–42, 156
central Fuerteventura 83
Gran Canaria 133
Lanzarote 109, 126
the North 63
the South 105
snorkelling 27
Sotavento 90–91
the South 85–106
accommodation 103–104
Cofete 98–99
Costa Calma 86, 90, 92, 96, 150
eating out 100–102
entertainment 106
Jandía Playa 86, 92, 96–97
La Lajita Oasis Park 22, 25, 31, 93–95
La Pared 86, 96
map 86–87
Morro Jable 86, 97–98
Playas de Jandía 90–92
shopping 105
three-day itinerary 88–89
Spanish Foreign Legion 75
speed limits 38
sports and activities
boat trips 52, 64, 84, 106
bodyboarding 22, 64
bowling 22
diving 23, 27, 42, 64, 84, 106
fishing 26, 64, 106
go-karting 84
golf 42, 84, 106

horseriding 84
jet skiing 64, 106
kite flying 23
kiteboarding 12, 13, 42, 64, 106
motorbike tours 84
mountain biking 84
quad bikes 64, 84
snorkelling 27
surfing 13–14, 22–23, 42, 64
swimming 91, 151
tennis 42, 106
walking and hiking 84, 115
waterskiing 106
whale and dolphin spotting 26, 64
windsurfing 12, 22, 42, 64, 84, 106
squirrels 25, 152
SS *American Star* 28–29, 33
stamps 157
straw hats 83
student travellers 158
submarine trips 27, 84, 106
sun safety 158
Superlative Fuerteventura 32–34
surfing 13–14, 22–23, 42, 64
swimming 91, 151

tapas 21, 40
Taro de Tahiche 120–121
tattoo shops 42
taxis
  Fuerteventura 36, 37
  Gran Canaria 129
Tefia 146
  Ecomuseo de La Alcogida 33, 66, 74, 146
Teguise 110, 118–119
  Casa Cuartel 118
  Castillo de Santa Barbara 119

Convento de San Francisco 118
Convento de Santo Domingo 118, 119
Iglesia de Nuestra Señora de Guadalupe 118
Palacio del Marqués 118, 119
Palacio Spínola 118, 119
telephones 157
tennis 42, 106
Tetir 149
Thomas, Ben 31
Timanfaya National Park 110, 114–115
time differences 155, 156
timeshare 38
tipping 40, 157
Tiscamanita 149
toilets 158
Tostón Tower 55
tourism 8
tourist information
  Fuerteventura 36–37
  Gran Canaria 129
  Lanzarote 109
tourist offices abroad 154–155
trepanning 133
Tuineje 17

Unamuno, Miguel 75, 76, 146

Valle de Santa Inés 8, 147
Valley of 1000 Palms 121
Vega de Río Palmas 77, 148
  Ermita de La Virgen de la Peña 17, 77
vegetarian food 20–21, 40
views of Fuerteventura 32–33
views of Lanzarote 123
Villa Tabaiba Galeria de Arte 50

Villa Winter 98–99
Villaverde 44, 56–57, 145
  Cueva Villaverde 56
  Hotel Rural Mahoh 56, 60, 145
  La Rosita 56–57
Volcan de Bayuyo 33, 145
volcanic activity 114–115, 116, 117, 140, 142, 143

walking and hiking 84, 115
walks and drives
  coast-to-coast 150–152
  Isla de Lobos 138–141
  north and central Fuerteventura 145–149
  Sendero de Bayuyo 142–144
water park 22, 49
waterskiing 106
websites 154
whale and dolphin spotting 26, 64
wildlife 24–25, 26, 139, 152
wildlife souvenirs 158
wind farm 150
Windmill Intrepretation Centre 78
windmills 7, 55–56, 73
windsurfing 12, 22, 42, 64, 84, 106
wines and spirits 21, 41, 109, 120
Winter, Gustav 99

yacht charter 106
Yaiza 110

zocos 120
zoo
  Jandía Playa 96–97
  Oasis Park 93–94

Picture Credits

The Automobile Association wishes to thank the following photographers and libraries for their assistance in the preparation of this book:
Front and Back Cover (t) AA World Travel Library/James A Tims; (ct) AA World Travel Library/Clive Sawyer; (cb) AA World Travel Library/Clive Sawyer; (b) AA World Travel Library/James A Tims; Spine AA World Travel Library/Steve Day
BRIDGEMAN ART LIBRARY West Coast of Africa, from Lisbon to Sierra Leone, from 'Atlas c Toutes les Parties Connues du Globe Terrestre' by Guillaume Raynal (1713-96) published Geneva, 1780 (coloured engraving), Bonne, Charles Marie Rigobert (1727-95)/Private Collection, Ken Welsh/Bridgeman Art Library 9bg; FLPA 24b; © DACS, 2005 116, 117t, 117 MARY EVANS PICTURE LIBRARY 9c, 10bg, 10t; NATURE PICTURE LIBRARY 26c; NHPA 26b; PHOTODISC 12/13t, 12c, 14l, 14r, 14b, 23t; TopFoto (www.topfoto.co.uk) 9t
The remaining photographs are held in the Association's own library (AA WORLD TRAVEL LIBRARY) and were taken by JAMES A TIMS with the exception of 11c, 127, 128, 129, 129b 131, 132b, 133t, 133b which were taken by PETE BENNETT; 18t which was taken by MICHELLE CHAPLOW; 5, 7t, 13t, 13b, 19t, 21bl, 23b, 25b, 27b, 32/33t, 34c, 34b, 48t, 65, 68c, 68b, 69t, 69c, 70c, 72t, 75b, 89c, 91t, 92ct, 92c, 112c, 112b, 117t, 117c, 120b, 121l 123, 139, 145l, 148, 151 which were taken by STEVE DAY; 2, 6/7bg, 6b, 7c, 8bg, 8t, 18b, 19 20t, 32c, 35, 66bl, 70b, 76b, 77, 86, 110, 112t, 122, 130, 134, 145 which were taken by CLIVE SAWYER and 26/27 which was taken by STEVE WATKINS
Abbreviations for term appearing above (t) top; (b) bottom: (l) left; (r) right; (c) centre; (bg background

Questionnaire

Dear Traveller

Your comments, opinions and recommendations are very important to us. Please help us to improve our travel guides by taking a few minutes to complete this simple questionnaire.

You do not need a stamp (unless posted outside the UK). If you do not want to remove this page from your guide, then photocopy it or write your answers on a plain sheet of paper.

Send to: The Editor, Spiral Guides, AA World Travel Guides, FREEPOST SCE 4598, Basingstoke RG21 4GY.

Your recommendations...

We always encourage readers' recommendations for restaurants, night-life or shopping – if your recommendation is used in the next edition of the guide, we will send you a FREE AA Spiral Guide of your choice. Please state below the establishment name, location and your reasons for recommending it.

_____

_____

_____

_____

_____

Please send me AA Spiral _____
(see list of titles inside the back cover)

About this guide...

Which title did you buy?

_____ AA Spiral

Where did you buy it? _____

When? m m / y y

Why did you choose an AA Spiral Guide? _____

_____

_____

_____

Did this guide meet your expectations?

Exceeded ☐ Met all ☐ Met most ☐ Fell below ☐

Please give your reasons _____

_____

_____

_____

_____

continued on next page...

Were there any aspects of this guide that you particularly liked?

_____

_____

_____

_____

_____

Is there anything we could have done better?

_____

_____

_____

_____

About you...

Name (Mr/Mrs/Ms) _____

Address _____

_____ **Postcode** _____

Daytime tel no _____ **email** _____

Please _only_ give us your email address and mobile phone number if you wish to hear from
us about other products and services from the AA and partners by email or text or mms.

Which age group are you in?

Under 25 ☐   25–34 ☐   35–44 ☐   45–54 ☐   55–64 ☐   65+ ☐

How many trips do you make a year?

Less than one ☐   One ☐   Two ☐   Three or more ☐

Are you an AA member? Yes ☐   No ☐

About your trip...

When did you book? mm/ y y   **When did you travel?** mm/ y y

How long did you stay? _____

Was it for business or leisure? _____

Did you buy any other travel guides for your trip? ☐ Yes   ☐ No

If yes, which ones? _____

_____

**Thank you for taking the time to complete this questionnaire. Please send it to us as soon
as possible, and remember, you do not need a stamp (unless posted outside the UK).**